Scattering Seed in Teaching

Scattering Seed in Teaching

Walking with Christ in the Field
of Learning and Education

BRIAN PICKERD

Foreword by Michael Pasquale

WIPF & STOCK · Eugene, Oregon

SCATTERING SEED IN TEACHING
Walking with Christ in the Field of Learning and Education

Wipf & Stock
An Imprint of Wipf and Stock Publishers
199 W. 8th Ave., Suite 3
Eugene, OR 97401

www.wipfandstock.com

PAPERBACK ISBN 13: 978-1-4982-3869-4
HARDCOVER ISBN 13: 978-1-4982-3871-7

Manufactured in the U.S.A.   01/13/2016

To family for encouraging me

To friends for listening to me

To my students for teaching me

To my God for continuously filling me

The task of the modern educator is not to cut down jungles, but to irrigate deserts.

—C. S. LEWIS, *THE ABOLITION OF MAN*

Contents

Foreword

JESUS OF NAZARETH WAS known by many titles—Messiah, Lord . . . and Teacher. The Jesus-as-teacher motif is found throughout the pages of the Gospels. He was a master educator and was able to connect with people through metaphor and parables. When we read about Jesus the teacher, we get a glimpse of his overwhelming love and care for people. This is clearly displayed in his Sermon on the Mount in the Gospel of Matthew.

Teaching is an honorable profession; rewarding, yet full of challenges. Teachers are vital to the growth and education of men, women, and children. *Scattering Seed* is written for teachers, those with a calling to teach and to live out their God-given vocation. This is a thought-provoking and inspiring book for both the novice and veteran educator. The scope of this book is not necessarily limited to those who teach in a traditional school setting, but also relates to those who teach in a university, church, or home.

I have had the privilege of knowing Brian Pickerd since he started teaching foreign language and education courses at Cornerstone University. He continues to teach German and French at a local public high school. Our friendship has grown over the years as we have many shared interests, ranging from international travel, to raising culturally intelligent children, to navigating the use of technology in the classroom. Brian practices what he preaches; he is a gifted teacher and a natural storyteller. He has helped inspire both current and future teachers by spending time with them. He loves to share winsome and engaging stories in a variety of contexts, such as in the classroom with students, over a cup of coffee with a colleague, and now on the written pages of this book with his readers.

Many of the stories in this book took place on Leonard Street, just a short distance from the campus of Cornerstone University. I have passed the Pickerd homestead many times over the years, often amazed at how it remained the same despite the changing landscape around it. You will be introduced to this farm and to its inhabitants, his grandparents.

The interactions between Brian and his grandparents are reminiscent of the stories told by the agrarian poet and philosopher Wendell Berry. In his writings Berry expresses the importance of farmers (particularly local family farmers) as nurturers. These farmers are in touch with the earth and lovingly care for it for the benefit of their families, their communities, and ultimately the whole of society. This is contrasted with those who exploit the earth for their own gain. They are out of touch with what constitutes a healthy culture. Brian makes a similar analogy between farmers and teachers as those who nurture. Just as his grandfather tended and cared for his piece of earth, so too must teachers care for their students. Nurture and care can shine through even in situations where teachers cannot be open about their faith.

Scattering Seed reads like a modern parable for teachers. We can take the principles and ideas presented in this book and apply them to our own teaching context. The illustrations are meaningful in helping us see how to do that. The reflection questions are a vital step in the application process.

Engaging with the ideas in this book has been an important step in my developmental process as a teacher. I encourage you to read through this book slowly, yet purposefully. Learn from a master teacher and be inspired!

Michael Pasquale, PhD
Author (with Nathan L. K. Bierma) of *Every Tribe and
Tongue: A Biblical Vision for Language in Society*
Grand Rapids, Michigan

Preface

THE PARABLE OF THE SOWER
(MATTHEW 13:1–23 NIV)

THAT SAME DAY JESUS went out of the house and sat by the lake. Such large crowds gathered around him that he got into a boat and sat in it, while all the people stood on the shore. Then he told them many things in parables, saying: "A farmer went out to sow his seed. As he was scattering the seed, some fell along the path, and the birds came and ate it up. Some fell on rocky places, where it did not have much soil. It sprang up quickly, because the soil was shallow. But when the sun came up, the plants were scorched, and they withered because they had no root. Other seed fell among thorns, which grew up and choked the plants. Still other seed fell on good soil, where it produced a crop—a hundred, sixty or thirty times what was sown. Whoever has ears, let them hear."

The disciples came to him and asked, "Why do you speak to the people in parables?"

He replied, "Because the knowledge of the secrets of the kingdom of heaven has been given to you, but not to them. Whoever has will be given more, and they will have an abundance. Whoever does not have, even what they have will be taken from them. This is why I speak to them in parables:

'Though seeing, they do not see;
    though hearing, they do not hear or understand.'

In them is fulfilled the prophecy of Isaiah:
'You will be ever hearing but never understanding;
   you will be ever seeing but never perceiving.
For this people's heart has become calloused;
   they hardly hear with their ears,
   and they have closed their eyes.
Otherwise they might see with their eyes,
   hear with their ears,
   understand with their hearts
and turn, and I would heal them.'

But blessed are your eyes because they see, and your ears because they hear. For truly I tell you, many prophets and righteous people longed to see what you see but did not see it, and to hear what you hear but did not hear it.

"Listen then to what the parable of the sower means: When anyone hears the message about the kingdom and does not understand it, the evil one comes and snatches away what was sown in their heart. This is the seed sown along the path. The seed falling on rocky ground refers to someone who hears the word and at once receives it with joy. But since they have no root, they last only a short time. When trouble or persecution comes because of the word, they quickly fall away. The seed falling among the thorns refers to someone who hears the word, but the worries of this life and the deceitfulness of wealth choke the word, making it unfruitful. But the seed falling on good soil refers to someone who hears the word and understands it. This is the one who produces a crop, yielding a hundred, sixty or thirty times what was sown."

Acknowledgments

I CANNOT FIND THE appropriate words to thank the many people who have supported the work of this book, many without necessarily knowing that they were doing so:

My wife, who listens to my endless sharing of interesting paragraphs and pages of other books and indulges my need to talk about them; my children, who have endured untold numbers of conversations connected with this book; my friends and colleagues in education who have read and critiqued pieces or the entirety of *Scattering Seed in Teaching*; my parents and sister for their deep support and encouragement.

Dr. Michael Pasquale, who also wrote the foreword to this book, I thank you for your motivation to restart my writing and for your ongoing support and suggestions. Mark Hetherington, my friend and spiritual co-mentor, I give you my gratitude for reading, editing, challenging, and discussing each word of each page with me.

Completion of this project would not have been accomplished without the years of teaching and learning opportunities given to me, the many colleagues (local and further afield), and the wonderful students who have been soil, seed, and plants.

Finally (and again), to my caring, loving, and supportive wife, Rachel: my deepest gratitude. Your encouragement when I wondered about the purpose of this project, your love in the midst of life's struggles, and your faith ongoing are a testimony to your dedication as my life mate as we work in life's garden together.

Introduction

. . . and in his teaching said: "Listen! A farmer went out to sow his seed. As he was scattering the seed, some fell along the path, and the birds came and ate it up. Some fell on rocky places, where it did not have much soil. It sprang up quickly, because the soil was shallow. But when the sun came up, the plants were scorched, and they withered because they had no root. Other seed fell among thorns, which grew up and choked the plants, so that they did not bear grain. Still other seed fell on good soil. It came up, grew and produced a crop, multiplying thirty, sixty, or even a hundred times."

—MARK 4:2B–8

The body is a unit, though it is made up of many parts; and though all its parts are many, they form one body.

—1 CORINTHIANS 12:12

But you are a chosen people, a royal priesthood, a holy nation, a people belonging to God, that you may declare the praises of him who called you out of darkness into his wonderful light.

—1 PETER 2:9

SCATTERING SEED IN TEACHING

ONE FALL DAY, MANY years ago, a class I was teaching had just finished an extremely difficult unit. I wanted to give my students a foreign language break before jumping into the next unit, which would be even more challenging. So I decided on a thought activity that would achieve two goals: the first was to get the class talking while letting me get to know them better; the other was to encourage the students to think about the importance of communication. To achieve this I wrote a historically relevant and thought-provoking quote on the board. It stated, "How fortunate for the leaders that men do not think" (my translation) (Was für ein Glück für die Regierenden, daß die Menschen nicht denken).[1] Through the quote I hoped to draw the class into a conversation that would challenge them at multiple levels, offer them a platform for expressing themselves, and through it all cause them to think on a larger scale.

My challenge to the class was to read the quote and share their insights into how one could understand it. Because I didn't want to influence the conversation on the front end, I did not tell them the name of the author. They started by guessing the author before trying to understand the meaning. The answers I heard revealed much about the students in my class. They tossed out the names of famous leaders from four different continents and shared several well thought-out interpretations of the quote. After several minutes of conversation, one student looked at me quizzically and asked me for the author of the quote. Though I wanted to wait a bit before doing so, I told them then that the quote came from Adolf Hitler.

The way in which the class received the information was very mature. No one made accusations or strange comments about other people's guesses or interpretations. Some nodded and admitted that they had thought the author might have been Hitler, but they didn't feel confident enough to come out and say so. Others were surprised, because of the contrast between the author and the people they had guessed. The one person in the class who

1. Janssen, "Was für ein Glück."

guessed correctly nodded and gave a small explanation to support his answer.

This discussion, which had the intent of tapping into the students' thoughts, did just that. It also quickly segued away from my intended path. A new conversation began, one about people's different roles in life, how people discover their paths, how beliefs and upbringings influence a person's professional direction, and how we can use our lives . . . to a positive end or an irresponsible one. What I had hoped would become a good discussion turned into much more.

In the midst of a now class-led discussion, my thoughts turned inward as the questions that the students were asking each other turned on me. I began to ask myself about the roles I was playing in life, how my upbringing and beliefs had influenced my professional direction, how and if I was using my life to a positive end. Was I? Or, was it possible that I was being irresponsible with it? What was happening?

For several days after that class, I continued pondering these questions. I could not erase the thoughts from my head. The discussion that day and the questions it raised have given rise to this book.

When I started teaching nearly twenty years ago, I hadn't made a full connection between a person's worldview and its application to the entirety of one' life . . . including the professional life. In hindsight I realize that God was still working on me in this area. I had moved into education from another profession and, as I quickly learned, into an entirely new world of communication and influence. In my first profession I had dealt entirely with business professionals. Shifting into a secondary English and foreign language classroom taught me that I needed to change more than just how I thought, communicated, and operated. I had to plan in an entirely new way. As a new teacher I spent most of my energy like other new teachers do, trying to stay a day, if not a full week, ahead of my classes. As a result I took far too little time to stop and ponder the larger picture of how my presence in the room was benefitting my students beyond the subjects I taught, let alone how my professional work was feeding into God's eternal picture.

Now, years later, I have learned the importance of asking these questions regularly. Like I said, this wasn't the case at the beginning though. It has been a process, and I understand now how necessary it was for me to work through this process and learn from it. Nonetheless, a part of me sometimes is still tempted by the question, "What if I had learned my lesson sooner? Is there some opportunity that I may have missed? What if I had seen the bigger picture earlier and been aware of something larger than my own small sphere of influence?"

As the Holy Spirit shifted my attention, I began waking to a new reality: the purpose of my personal life carried over into my professional life in education. In fact it was all part of the same purpose, but it extended beyond teaching language in secondary schools, beyond volunteering in elementary school and Sunday school classes, even beyond teaching university courses; it reached far beyond sharing my practical life experiences with them. I recognized that being a part of the body of Christ meant that God had called me to play a role in that body, one whose focus was on giving him glory in and through everything I did. He had called me to be a part of the redemptive work of his body. He had given me a set of gifts as well as a professional calling. He had placed me in a specific role with a task, and he was inviting me to live and move among a specific population and use the gifts and skill sets he had given me. He called me to be a reflection of himself to those around me by how I live. He was calling me to acknowledge my place in the priesthood of believers and "declare the praises of the one who called you out of darkness into the wonderful light" (1 Peter 2:9). He was asking me to join in his work of healing in this world through the work I received. He was asking me to scatter seed.

This revelation took me by storm. I hadn't taken to heart that this was part the big picture of what it meant to be a believer. I had not made the connection between my faith calling and my professional role as a teacher. I had sensed it, having heard sermon messages about our faith walk being all encompassing, but despite the Sunday morning lessons the message hadn't sunk in. It hadn't occurred to me that God had placed me in a profession with the intent of using me to share his love, his beauty, and his healing through it. I hadn't paid attention to the myriad ways in which teachers reflect who they are and what they believe to students, to colleagues, and to community. Nor had I internalized the implications of doing so. Not only that, but I stood in the midst of an educational conversation held by many religious people, of sorts, but in which religion's role is often called into question. In time it slowly became clear to me that God was changing me in a way that would allow me to contribute to this conversation. Furthermore, he was removing the blocks that had kept him from doing his work through me.

As I listened, I heard God's "still small voice" in this area of my life. As I did, I recognized the work he had started in me, and that work has entirely changed how I see my calling as a Christian . . . and my role as a teacher. God shifted my understanding of who he is, and therefore who I am. he reached into my heart and taught me a deeper understand of the propensities that he had given me. Furthermore, he started to show me what he intended to do with them and how I needed to trust him to use me. I needed to understand that I was a sower in the middle of a field, and my purpose was to give him glory through how I do my work. The more I listened, the more God showed me who I am as an individual, as a teacher, a colleague, and a community member. He began to open my eyes to what the Holy Spirit was doing in me and why. Furthermore, he gave me increased clarity to see the great amount of work ahead of me, as I tried to understand the nature of being a Christian teacher in a place that at certain times allows the discussion of God, in general, but draws a separation line from talking about it in specific.

Being aware of the political struggles existent in the field of education, I have listened more closely to the various interpretations of church and state separation. In doing so I have recognized that each interpretation desires, according to its philosophical underpinnings, to work toward the welfare of the students. In the midst of this experience, I have continued to gain another sense of purpose in my teaching. It is more than training my students in language, experiences, and skills for their futures. It is more than encouraging them in their development of self and finding unity in their learning. It is to share healing and light with them through the work that I have received to do. It is, in fact, to reflect God's care and compassion to my students, colleagues, and community. My purpose was and is to scatter seed.

This book, being a part of that seed scattering, aims at encouraging you to scatter seed too. It is intended, first and foremost, to be a book of encouragement to action for you as a future or current teacher, whatever the context might be. But, in an effort to encourage you, I also want to share some of the lessons I have learned about the scope of Christian mission and challenge you to consider its connection with how you live through your work in the field of education. From there, I want to encourage you to recognize that, given those two pictures, you as a teacher fall into a variety of roles, each with specific responsibilities. These roles and responsibilities find their roots in your personal spiritual life. They play out in every aspect of your work in the classroom and, in many cases, beyond the classroom into the community. The second purpose is to challenge you to action, taking the thoughts and experiences found in the individual chapters and prayerfully seeking out where and to what extent God will use you as a teacher (depending on your context) as he pours himself out through your work.

The insights shared in this book come from real-life teaching experiences. The interviews and observations shared have been gleaned from a wide spectrum of teaching environments, and the people interviewed and observed come from a variety of schools— public, private, inner city, suburban, rural. The information shared represents private and public, low-, medium-, and upper-income schools and families as well as a mixture of socioethnic groups. I have intentionally changed the names and details of individual personalities to maintain the anonymity of the people from whom

I have learned and who have directly shared their thoughts and experiences with me. The vignettes that I will share are intended to be an encouragement and a challenge as well as to give root to the overall message. They will be intermingled with statistics and quotes from a variety of previous thinkers and writers to build the case for teachers acting through their lives as educators to give God glory and offer an appropriate picture of Christianity by living as Christ did, caring for those around him and placing the needs of others before his sense of personal comfort. All of this works toward the end of helping teachers to scatter seed.

Though the first intent of this book was to reach out to Christian teachers in a traditional context, the material reaches beyond that audience. What it communicates can just as well speak to youth leaders, Sunday school teachers, homeschool parents, professors, counselors, spiritual leaders, and parents. Each leads and teaches. Each depends on relationship to do so. Each ties in with our overall faith calling.

This book follows an agricultural metaphor, hence the title. Some chapters are more theoretically weighted, while others carry a more practical purpose. Throughout the book, I lean on the power of story and example to drive the teaching. Through the reflection and discussion questions I challenge you to find yourself along the passage of learning and teaching, growing and helping others to grow. And wherever you personally prescribe to this worldview or not, I invite you to listen to the broad-scoped wisdom in what is being communicated and understand that wherever you stand in your spiritual walk, it will certainly show through in how you move and speak and teach. For all of us scatter seed, intentionally or unintentionally. So for the sake of caring for our students, colleagues, and communities . . .

I invite you to join in *Scattering Seed*.

1

Tools for the Taking
The History of Seed Scattering

Mission and Witness: No matter how much we must struggle, the focus is not us. It is not other people. It is God, and reflecting him to those around us. Keep that focus!

ONE DAY WHEN I was twelve, my dad informed me that he had to run some errands, and that I would be coming with him. He wouldn't tell me exactly where we were going, but dads are often that way when their children insist on knowing everything. Though I pursued the matter further, he simply repeated that we had to run some errands. The so-called errands ended up bringing us to Sears. My thought was that I had been brought on the trip to get me out of my mother's hair while my dad bought himself some new tools, and I was certain that I was right when we turned into the ratchet aisle. But then my dad surprised me by asking me what I thought about the forty-piece tool sets. He wanted my opinion, which was unusual, and I couldn't understand why. The

8

background of the matter is that for the previous several months I had been doing the same things that most boys do at that age. I had been borrowing my dad's tools to tinker around. I had been taking apart and sometimes accidentally fixing things around our yard—bicycles, swing sets, and yard tools. My father had, unbeknownst to me, been watching me and decided that the time had come for me to have my own set of tools. He meant for me to stop playing around with the idea of work and start working. Rather than borrowing wrenches and screwdrivers and forgetting them in the lawn or in the middle of the garage to rust or be run over by the car, he planned to present me with my own tool set.

As it turned out, something about me changed once I had my own set of tools. I took ownership of them and learned to become more responsible than I had been with my father's wrenches and screwdrivers. I discovered how to use them properly, and I started to help fix things around the house—even some that hadn't been broken before I placed my hands on them. I had to ask a lot of questions along the way (I still do to this day), but finally I came into the position where I could do some useful work around our home. As my realization of this grew, I began to invest more in my family, because I had learned that I had something to contribute . . . and I wanted to make my dad proud of me. It felt great because, for the first time, I recognized how important it was for me to do what I could—especially since I had received the gift of my own set of tools. As time passed the meaning of this period of my life grew more deeply in my heart.

Ephesians 4:11–12 talks to us about this. The verses draw a wonderful connection between the gifts that God gives us and the work he wants us to do. "It was he who gave some to be apostles, some to be prophets, some to be evangelists, and some to be pastors and teachers, to prepare God's people for works of service, so that the body of Christ may be built up." God wants us to recognize this connection and look at our talents and interests in life. The purpose is for us to use them to reflect God and join him in his work of building. God wants each of us to pay attention to his voice and listen to the call he has given us. He looks for our response. He desires for us to follow his will, not just during the weekly worship service or when we are speaking with other Christians. He wants to see us doing his will in our daily interactions as well.

Reflect and discuss:

1. *Reread the last few sentences and think about them. When is it hard to recognize what they are suggesting and apply the lessons to our work?*

MISSION

For teachers there are specific ramifications involved in following our gifts and calling, especially given our profession and the specific responsibilities connected with it. God gives us a group of tools: a penchant for learning, a desire to share what we have learned with others, and an ability to present in a way that helps others learn. He also gives us a craving to help and to show. Because of this combination of tools, we encounter the people we meet each day in a very specific way. If the people we teach see us as loving, fair, compassionate, and trustworthy, they tend to want to listen to us; they seek out our opinion. They ask us about important matters in life, and they take our answers to heart. Knowing this holds great significance though. And so the theme of gifts and talents easily translates itself into the primary focus of this section, *mission*. We need a solid understanding of mission, as it will help guide us as Christian teachers, regardless of the setting in which we are called to teach.

God's calling to you to work as a teacher implies that he is also inviting you live out that professional calling in direct connection to your larger calling in his mission. The quandary for so many of us Christian teachers is that we struggle with internalizing our calling to his mission, and therefore, unknowingly, we often fail at living it out in our professional life. But what is that mission? Understanding what God's mission is and how we are a part of it every day is central to our life in general as well as to our vocation as teachers. It will help us to better wrap our minds around the great implications of our call to teach. It will help us understand the larger field we are in, the roles we might be called to play, our responsibilities, and the work God has given us to do in and beyond the classroom. So let's draw this connection! Let's look into the picture of mission that the Bible gives us and see if we can find our place in that mission!

There seems to be an expectation among some Christians that everyone grasps the meaning of mission, but perhaps that is a mistake. Mission has specific meaning and purpose. It is at once simple and complicated and therefore often misunderstood. The word itself causes many to conjure up thoughts of faraway places and underprivileged people. We imagine courageous missionaries traveling to developing-world countries and delivering the gospel to people who have never heard of Christ. We picture church groups spending Saturday evenings at inner-city soup kitchens serving meals to the homeless. We think of week-long service learning adventures for high school youth groups. We think of people sharing how many they have "lead to Christ." These initiatives promote aspects of God's mission, but we do injustice to that mission when we limit our picture there. His plan is all-encompassing. As 1 Peter 1:15–16 tells us, "But just as he who called you is holy, so be holy in all you do; for it is written: 'Be holy, because I am holy.'" God is telling us here to *be* holy (set apart for his work), not just to act holy or put on a show when a set of circumstances demands it. We cannot limit our life of mission to certain corners of our existence or times on our calendars. It needs to permeate *everything* that we do, say, think, and are.

God gives us his Word to guide us in our lives. Through all of Scripture he shows us his mission. Each chapter and book speaks of God's work in the lives of his people, whether it is through history, parable, poetry, or prophecy. Senior and Stuhlmueller suggest that "The entire Bible . . . lays the foundation for mission."[1] In fact, the first words of Genesis 1:1, "In the beginning God created the heavens and the earth," show the beginning of God's mission, and the balance of God's Word continues the story until Revelation's final "Amen."

When God created the world, he also created a garden. This garden represented God's provision for the people he had made. It also represented his presence with them. God gave man and woman the job of caring for creation. It was their job to take care of the garden. That man and woman had fair access to every kind of food except one, because it represented knowledge that was too great for them to grasp. God allowed the fruit to hang in plain view though. Strangely enough, this showed God's love for humankind,

---

1. Senior and Stuhlmueller, *Biblical Foundations for Mission*, 315.

for in the process of giving us life God also gives us free will to listen and accept his love, or not. God offered his clear instruction to avoid the fruit; he also gave clear explanation of the outcome of disobedience. (Genesis 2:17) Nonetheless man and wife fell together. They immediately realized the outcome of their sin together and they lived with the consequences.

At that point, the direction of God's mission shifted. God had created humankind and offered them a life of direct contact to his creator, in his garden—in his presence—but the fall resulted in humanity's inability to go on enjoying God in that garden. Rather than giving up on his creation, though, God set a process in action, one that Van Rheenen refers to as "God's desire to reconcile sinful humanity to himself."[2] In the process, God keeps showing his love by moving toward his creation, even if humanity's movement is effectively away from him. The Bible undeniably displays God's love as he pursues his ongoing work to reconcile his people. We see two major movements in this activity, and a closer study of Scripture will increase our awareness of God's mission and how it can play out in our lives. Let's take a peek!

OLD TESTAMENT MISSION

Throughout the Old Testament, God pursued his people. He made his covenant with Abraham in chapter 12 of Genesis. He promised to build a nation through him and bless that nation greatly, and he did just that. "Abraham, I will make of thee a great nation, and I Will bless thee, and make thy name great; and thou shalt be a blessing: and I will bless them that bless thee, and curse them that curse thee: and in thee shall all the families of earth be blessed." In Genesis 12:2–3 God established his people in order to lift them up and give them everything they could possibly need. His plan was to give them such an abundance that they would not go wanting. He promised to protect Abraham and bless the nation through him. In return he appeared to ask his people primarily

---

2. Van Rheenen, *Missions*, 21.

for two things: obedience to his law and hearts that listen to his voice. The centripetal (drawing inward from the outside) nature of God's mission with the Israelites was intended to work in such an obvious way that other peoples would see the beauty of a life in harmony with God and in relationship with him, and desire the same relationship.

Despite God's ongoing love and care for them, his people repeatedly fell, and each time they did God reminded them of the consequences of their disobedience. As a loving father, God refused to give up on his people; he continued giving them opportunities to repent and return to him. He did so through the building of the ark of the covenant and the temple as places where his presence would reside for his people. He even sent prophets to speak to his people directly about the present and the future, but Israel continued to regress, even after they saw the fruits of their repentance and relationship with God, even after hearing about the calamities that came though ongoing disobedience. The people that God had offered a covenant simply could not bring themselves to rely on divine leading. So, as a result, God's mission shifted again, and a new covenant came.

IN CHRIST

This shift came in the person of Jesus. Once God began his work through him on Earth, the mission focus that we see in the Old Testament took on a slightly different bent. God never stopped pursuing people, but the blessing that had been centered on Israel expanded. God maintained his covenant with the Israelites, but he extended his hand to non-Jews as well, just as he had said in Isaiah. We see this in Simeon's words to God in Luke 2:30–32: "For my eyes have seen your salvation, which you have prepared in the sight of all people, a light for salvation to the Gentiles and for glory to your people Israel." He spoke these words when Christ was presented in the temple. Years before Jesus ever spoke his first adult words, his ministry was foreshadowed in his presence.

[Handwritten margin note:] I don't think of God shifting his plan. It was always his plan to do in this way (to send Jesus & get all people). He foreknew how he would accomplish each step of 1 plan!

14

Once Jesus began his public ministry, he went out and called disciples who would follow him. He trained them to go out to other people, other nations. Jesus represented God's mission as it took on a new nature. He first worked outward from a center, beginning with one group (Israel) that would draw others in from the outside. God then worked through Jesus and sent disciples (and us) out among other people to minister to them where they were (and are). The outward appearance of the mission's face changed. It was no longer primarily centripetal, but now centrifugal (working outward from the center) as well.

In Matthew 4:19 Jesus said, "Come, follow me, and I will make you fishers of men." He wasn't simply calling people to follow him and study his word. Jesus called young followers under his yolk (or teaching) as a group of disciples whom he intended to teach. As they followed and learned from him, they responded to his care and love and worked to be like him. This is very important for us to note as teachers. It means that the disciples left behind their old understanding of life (the one that focused on themselves and their earthly wants) and spent their days focusing on becoming like their teacher, in thought, in word, and in deed. Christ's life and teaching drew people inward. It challenged, instructed, and encouraged them to become fishers of men.

Jesus shared his agape (love) with everyone—everyone—and he taught his disciples to do the same. He prepared them to go to the nations (beyond Israel) and show them the same healing love and compassion that they had seen in him. This model has been passed down from Christ, through the disciples and the early church, to us today. Christ's word, shown in the Gospels and the Epistles, offers us numerous examples of going out in acts of love, justice, and healing on God's behalf; and it speaks to us about how our work as teachers should look, how it can scatter seed.

TODAY

Christ's actions and words in the Gospels teach us about mission and witness. This is especially clear in the Great Commission and the resulting activity of the disciples and the early church. They show us a model of how to live our lives as followers of Christ. First, Christ calls us to live as a family of believers (Ephesians 5) who live, work, and serve one another authentically. We don't do this because we will be seen and rewarded. We don't do this co-vertly, trying to sneak our worldview in under the radar. We go and live as Christ did, and we do this in response to Christ's love for us. We do so with the understanding that in glorifying God this way we will also allow others to experience Christ through our lives, knowingly or unknowingly. Second, Christ teaches us to extend the focus of ministry by caring for those outside the family of believers, reaching out and building relationships with them, blessing them by how we live, and praying for them. Third, through his teachings Christ instructs us, as believers, to spread seed, so to speak, everywhere we go. As the sower in Matthew 18, we should (by how we think, live, speak, and believe) scatter seed everywhere we go in trust that God will find the fertile soil and grow the seed where he desires.

This action should permeate our lives and our schedules. It should show through in everything we do, think, and say; with our congregation, in the home, in the classroom, on the sports field—everywhere. Scripture speaks to varying aspects of this. Peter en-courages his readers in that direction. In 1 Peter 4:10–11 we read that "Each one should use whatever gift he has received to serve others, faithfully administering God's grace in its various forms. If anyone speaks, he should do it as one speaking the very words of God. If anyone serves, he should do it with the strength God provides, so that in all things *God may be praised* . . ." Furthermore, in Colossians 3:23 Paul writes about the message of holy living in a way that clearly fits into the theme of mission and witness: "Whatever you do, work at it with all your heart, as working for the Lord, not for men . . ." There is no ambiguity in these words. God, speaking through these writers, is sending us out to work, something that sometimes requires great faith.

In going out and serving God and one another, we understand that our faith must inform our entire life: socially, academically, and otherwise. We understand that as we serve we may be seen as being different (although being noticed is not our principal reason for living as we do). We also understand that we need to be prepared to answer the questions that may result. ~~Our lives, after all,~~ *not what He very says* "preach the word" (2 Timothy 4:2), and we are called to "be prepared in season and out of season" (2 Timothy 4:2) because, if we are living Spirit-led lives, we will encounter a variety of reactions for an assortment of reasons. Some reactions might stem from curiosity. In other cases a reaction could stem from suspicion of our motives. Regardless of the reaction or its source, the Bible is clear that we must be "prepared": prepared to answer for our joy and **I need more preparation!* peace, prepared to answer questions about our faith, prepared with a Scriptural understanding of who we are and why we are called.

I don't mean to suggest that you must declare a major in theology and missions. Our task is as simple and as challenging as anything in life could ever be. It is simple because it is the only reaction that should come from our faithful following of Christ. It is a natural outflow of God's unconditional love for us reflected in our interactions with others and our thoughts about others. It is also impossibly difficult to do on our own, because so much of what this world teaches appears to stand in direct contrast to it. People who hold an absolute faith are often told, and not necessarily politely, to keep their "religion" to themselves. Christians are therefore called to speak (in word and action) in a certain way. Paul tells the Ephesians how believers should conduct themselves. In explaining what that means, he addresses our speech, challenging us to "Be very careful, then, how you live—not as unwise but as wise, making the most of every opportunity, because the days are evil . . . speaking to one another with psalms, hymns, and songs from the Spirit" (5:15–16, 19). Does this mean that we memorize Scripture in order to be prepared to deliver perfunctory mini-speeches to everyone we meet? It seems more likely to mean that keeping God's Word in our heart enables us to speak in a manner keeping with how Christ walked and spoke—full of grace and sincerity. That doesn't mean in a maudlin greeting-card tone and plastic smile; it means acting and using speech that is honest and full of love.

THE GREAT COMMISSION LEADING US TO THE FIELD

In Matthew 28:18–20 Jesus officially sent the disciples. This Jesus, to whom "all authority on heaven and on earth has been given," uses action verbs in his commissioning, one of which is "go." The disciples, and we, through our membership in the body of Christ, receive the message to move. Jesus tells us to go into the world, go into our circles of influence, go into our families, go wherever the Holy Spirit leads and reflect Christ. In speaking to his disciples in John 20:21, Christ tells us, "As the Father has sent me, so I am sending you." The entire notion is one of forward movement. Go out among the people, not huddling in the protection of the church community. The community has its purpose for support and growth, but "Go!" is centrifugal. Make contact! Build relationships! Live the Gospel! Love! Give God glory! Share beauty and healing! Go!

The entire movement of God's mission is one of progress. The family of believers has always been in motion, whether among a specific group of people over an extended period of time, or actually moving from one place to another as Paul did. And while we go, we are given a task, which Mark's account of Christ's commission shows.

Jesus commissioned his people in Mark 16:15 to go and preach the good news. He gave this task while also explaining that not everyone will believe. Taking the Matthew 28 verses together with Mark, we preach by example with our lives: by how we speak, act and react, by how we think, and how we love. The real preaching begins in our hearts, though; it starts with our relationship with and growth in Christ, which pours out into our demeanor and becomes outwardly visible. If we intend to obey Christ's charge in the Great Commission, then our hearts have to be in position so that the rest of who we are is informed by the Holy Spirit's influence.

Living through the Holy Spirit will draw attention, regardless of how quiet and subtle a person you are. You will be or become salt and light of the earth, once the Spirit begins working in you. You will become recognizable as that person who "seems to be different," and sooner or later someone is bound to be curious enough to ask you about it. After all, Psalms 34:5 tells us, "Those who look to him are radiant . . ." When the questions come though, how will you answer? What will you say? Will you be ready? You will be, if you are living in the Spirit and speaking the words that the Spirit gives you.

Depending upon your teaching context, openly sharing about your faith may or may not be permitted. If it is, do so with joy. If it is not, explain such. There is dishonesty in presuming to be an undercover evangelist. Our calling is, again, to give God glory by *how* we live and teach. If, however, you are directly asked about your faith, and the situation and context permit, share.

Some people cannot imagine ever sharing personal faith with another person. It seems far too stressful, not to mention awkward. It's true that not everyone has been given the gift of words. However, every Christian is called to be a *living* witness. Everyone who has experienced salvation and realized the state of his or her life before and after conversion can tell about that experience. In that sense we are all able to answer Christ's call to give an account for the hope we have. We simply share our story.

Certainly this is not the end of mission; it is the next beginning. Mission and witness carry the sole purpose of gathering people to Christ, but that is secondary. Our primary purpose in our life is to serve Christ and bring him glory. As the first question and answer of the Westminster Confession of Faith states, "What is the chief end of man? Man's chief end is to glorify God, and to enjoy him forever."[3] The mission of each Christian is to join God in his mission, bringing him glory through it.

And this brings us back to the beginning of this chapter, and the story. The set of tools that my father purchased for me had a set purpose. Teachers fit into the metaphor in more than one way. We

3. Westminster Short Catechism, question 1.

as Christians are the receivers of gifts of salvation. We are also the recipients of tools, tools that allow us to teach others to use theirs. We are at once the child playing around with the tools of another, and the Father who looks to instruct a child about how and when to use the various tools he or she has received. We are also met with two decisions. We are the child who must reach a conclusion about whether to receive his own tools as a gift and do something about them or continue playing at life. We can also be the father figure, and resolve to teach with fervor through our calling or go on watching others leave their borrowed tools to get lost and rust.

The mission is clear and the calling has been made. We have been called into a relationship and vocation. Now we must stand and look into the implications it has for us. The first perspective we will take is that of the very field in which we work our vocation as teachers.

2

Knowing the Field

Ask the former generation
and find out what their ancestors learned,
for we were born only yesterday and know nothing,
and our days on earth are but a shadow.

Will they not instruct you and tell you?
Will they not bring forth words from their understanding?

—JOB 8:8–10

You did not choose me, but I chose you and appointed you so
that you might go and bear fruit—fruit that will last—and so
that whatever you ask in my name the Father will give you.

—JOHN 15:16

ONE SPRING (I'M NOT certain how old I was . . . perhaps nine or
ten.), my father dropped me off on Saturdays to spend the morn-

ing with my grandparents while he put in some overtime hours at work. One particular Saturday stands out in my mind. When I ran into the kitchen Grandma wrapped her wet dishwashing hands around me in a hug and told me that Grandpa was out in the greenhouse waiting for me.

I raced down the stairs, without removing my shoes, and shot out the screen door to the plastic-wrapped wooden structure. There stood Grandpa with his massive hands covered in dirt. He turned his head like an owl and nodded to my presence. Then he wiped the earth from his fingers and offered me a hand. Grandpa saved his words for the right purpose and time. He told me it was time to look at the field. I knew better than to ask yet. Grandpa's method was "watch and learn." We walked over the field that he knew as well as the veins pulsing out of the back of his massive hands. Nonetheless, with each spring's thaw Grandpa looked at his field.

As we walked he looked at the weeds that pressed through. He would stop and stare at the soil now and again and sometimes gather some in his hand to sift between his fingers. Then he would thoughtfully nod and move on. This process took a while. I'm not sure how long. Time is confusing to all ages, especially to a nine- or ten-year-old. When we were done, though, Grandpa and I returned to the greenhouse for some more pre-planting work before heading to the house for lunch.

Grandpa's quiet method of teaching about plants and gardens often collided with my way of learning, because I learn by talking. So, as a talker eventually does, I gathered my words and asked, "Grandpa, why did we need to walk over all ten acres of your garden and stare at the dirt? And why did you pick up dirt, nod, and drop it?" Grandpa's answer was classic to those who knew him. It was short, to the point, and somewhat ironic in tone. "How else should I know what's in the dirt? An old farmer has to understand his garden so he knows what it needs." And he continued to move seedlings from one tray to another.

My grandfather farmed his entire life, in one context or another. I never had a clear view of his theology, for he was, as I hinted, a man of few words. Nonetheless, the understanding of life that he gained through his years in God's soil, and the lessons he taught his grandchildren while spending time with them in the field, have stood as a great metaphor for me.

As Jesus taught, he showed a perfect understanding of the field in which he planted. In the Gospels we read his words, explore his context, and gather a picture for how he wove his planting of spiritual seed with eternal wisdom. He knew the world he had created and how humanity had refocused the values of that world. He was intimately connected to the people whom he had made in his image, the people whom sin had corrupted. He came for them. He taught them. He lived in front of them, and he did it with thoughtfulness to the context of the time and place in which he taught.

As Christian teachers we have a calling on our lives to sow seeds of beauty and healing through our activity in the field of education. It is therefore of vital importance to understand something about that field. We need to walk around in it and look at the ground, survey the weeds, pick up some of the soil, and sift it around in our fingers. In other words we need to consider how education thinks. We need to understand what it values, what expectations it holds, what has contributed to its current state, and finally, we must see how our biblical values parallel the goals of education and can therefore bring beauty and healing there.

Reflect and discuss:

2. *How does society as a whole appear to view education?*

3. *How do you view it?*

4. *What values and goals does education appear to have?*

5. *What expectations are placed on it?*

6. *How do you understand all of this tying into us as Christian teachers?*

Grandpa and I hadn't been back in the greenhouse working for very long before my grandmother's famously loud, shaky call rang across the back yard from the kitchen window, "Don! Dinner!"(Dinner is what my grandparents called lunch.) Grandpa turned toward me and said the simple words, "I think dinner is ready," and we left the greenhouse to wash for lunch.

Once we were seated at the table, Grandma brought in the meal and prayed with us. It was then time to refuel from the morning's work and enjoy some conversation. I took the opportunity to ask the question that had been rolling around in my head for much of the morning while Grandpa and I were in the field. I looked at my grandfather and asked, "Grandpa, why do you need to walk around and look at the field every year? Why don't you just go out and plant the vegetables like everyone else does? Don't they just grow on their own?"

My question must have been timed right, because my grandfather turned toward me, put down his fork, and answered. "Brian, that dirt has been there for a long time, but I'm not the first person to work in it, and I'm not the only one using it now. The cars that drive down Leonard Street leave their fumes in the air. Then it rains, and the gas is in the soil. Planes fly overhead, and their fumes end up in the garden too. And who knows how much trash and oil were dumped in this ground before your grandma and I bought this place. Not everyone cares about this dirt. Not everyone understands it. They think they can just stick a seed in the ground and let it take care of itself. Dirt can't do everything, but it can grow food for a long time if you plant good seed and take care of it. A good farmer looks at his field every year to understand it. He's got to work with the soil that he has if he wants his plants to grow and give him vegetables that he can eat." Then his answer was done, and so without wasting any time he put his fork back in hand for another bite of dinner. This mini-seminar was perhaps the longest explanation my grandfather had given me up to that point, and now, years later, the wisdom comes pouring out.

Our field of education is similar to my grandfather's field. We teachers aren't the only factors exerting themselves there. Other influences affect the field in which we work every day. Some of them are currently at work while others remain left over from decades and centuries past. So, as good farmers, or teachers, we can benefit ourselves, our students, and our calling by taking a walk and looking over our field. For doing so places us in much better position to find our place there and grasp what the field requires of us . . . how we are to serve there. Let's go now and look around!

As we pointed out when discussing the history of the mission in the chapter 1, God planted the original garden. When he did this he gave us responsibility for its care. God made us to be the caretakers of his garden. Since the beginning we were planters and nurturers of the earth. And since the beginning we were made to know and have a relationship with God. Once sin entered into the world, though, we found ourselves separated from that original relationship we had with God. Ever since, we have been on a search to find that original relationship with him, to answer our questions of origin, seek out our purpose, and find our direction. In the spirit of this we have created programs of learning of all sorts in an effort to answer the questions that our hearts yearn to answer and lay out a plan for our direction in society and life. Each generation and each region of the world has, at one point or another, found the solution through some form of education. Depending on how people in a certain time and place determined their focus or interpreted the important questions that they wanted to answer, they created educational systems to match. The ancient Hebrews developed their system of teaching, which would bring the best to be rabbis. The Greeks started their lyceum and academies, etc. . . .

Over the course of time education has taken on a host of faces and purposes, all seeking to answer big questions and accomplish societal goals. From era to era, region to region, however, populations have come to differ in their purposes for education and therefore their approaches to it. One observation, though, can be consistently made. Education, in spite of its origin, has often functioned as a tool to serve the purposes of those with the power and intent to use it. It has been employed to honorable as well as dubious ends, and therefore its reputation has been both lauded and vilified. At various points in history, education, rather than searching for the answers to ultimate questions, was reserved for the privileged, creating a line of division between the upper echelons of society and the lower classes. In other times and places, the ruling classes instituted a more or less forced education and used it as a means of establishing order and maintaining the class structure. Today we observe a mixture of emotions flowing to the surface whenever the topic of education arises, and this has its reasons.

Reflect and discuss:

7. *Reread this last paragraph and consider its suggestions. What evidence do we see of this today?*

8. *How can Christians prepare to respond?*

The sociological role that education plays frequently leads to an "us versus them" mentality among educators, as well as between educators and individuals outside of the education system. Teachers sometimes develop a protective attitude when social, economic, and political strains turn the public eye on education and blame it for society's ills. For a Christian to develop such a polarizing mindset, though, is reactionary at best. For God offers us a longer perspective. He teaches us to watch and understand, rather than cast blind judgment. He tells us to be salt and light. He asks us to step back and look into the reasons why we see what we see, to look beneath the surface for the cause of the situation. For every current situation that we encounter now has its source in the past.

Looking back to history again, we observe a human phenomenon at work. Each generation intentionally or unintentionally espouses a certain philosophy, resulting from that generation's probing for answers to its problems and challenges. This probing frequently results in a proverbial finger being pointed at the preceding generation. Thinking about this tendency aids our discussion about the current field of education because it helps explain why such a critical public eye is placed on education and how education has come to appear the way it does. If we review the progression of thoughts from the last few hundred years leading up to the present, and consider their effects on education (both now and in the future), we can gain some insight into how to ask God to use us there.

Medieval Europe was much different from the West as we see it now. Texts of the time indicate an overall theocentric explanation of the world. It was a time during which science served as a path of inquiry for understanding God's creation. In the centuries following the Middle Ages, however, the purpose of science shifted. During the Enlightenment, science gained a new and different foothold, not so much as the supporter of a biblical explanation of life, but as *the* explanation of life itself, independent of a biblical, spiritual tie. A seemingly subtle notion on the surface, it proved vast in its scope. Religion was considered by most philosophers as a tool useful for keeping people moral. The Enlightenment's philosophical follower, modernity, continued the trend and produced an ongoing shift in the Western worldview.

The powers at play in this shift were not merely walking away from the biblical worldview, though. They were also reacting to the political powers of the time, powers that frequently misused religion. Royal families and heads of state, understanding the religious devotion of their subjects, repeatedly used that devotion as a tool to organize society in a way that benefitted themselves. Enlightenment minds rejected these abuses by the royal classes and the religion that they promoted at a time concurrent with their new discoveries in the sciences. As they grasped onto the new, they walked away from the old. The outcome was threefold: an observable move away from eternal matters toward the temporal, the public perspective downgrading God and replacing him with the intellect, and a struggle to create a plane of equality for people. From that point, science would increasingly provide the answers to questions of import. Moral and spiritual absolutes would often find themselves marginalized. They would come to be substituted by humankind and their intellect as the measuring stick of truth and right versus wrong. And, finally, the social hierarchy would be challenged and equality of citizens sought.

Education today still experiences the effects of this long trajectory. In some manners of speaking, the effects are beneficial. Yet not all changes benefit all people. This cultural rejection of absolutes lingers in educational conversation, at least as far as they hold any spiritual connection. We seek desperately to establish equality among individuals (something that God established "in the beginning"), yet we ascribe the idea to human ingenuity. Secularization has sought to remove God's name from the common language. Intellectual knowledge, rather than being ascribed to him, has replaced him; and education, the vehicle by which knowledge is said to travel, is advertised as the great equalizing factor.

In this environment parents understandably desire a promising future for the next generation. They seek opportunities for their children to gain a foothold in life. Local communities alike look to build hopes for their future, and entire nations compete in

29

a global economic race with hopes of winning. And in all of this, their eyes move toward a common means through which they all hope to achieve their goals. Here is where education finds itself in the spotlight as the public asks educators to deliver a solution.

As teachers, we must understand these things and stand ready to meet the challenges that they present. What exactly is our role in the calling to teach? We have an idea of what has been deposited on the field in the past, but how do we respond to it now?

We will break down the larger question in the individual chapters to follow. The simple answer, though, is that we teach students in a way that prepares them to compete in the marketplace, and that is indeed an important part of what we do. We would be remiss to ignore that fact. As Christians, though, we would also be irresponsible to leave matters there. For far more is at stake. Our task as teachers is about much more than the bundling and delivery of information. It is greater than a journey toward a career. It is also about the journey taken with the individuals whom we teach—a journey that at times seems temporal, but in the end is one that encourages eternal souls toward or away from their creator. Accepting this reality and looking more deeply, more compassionately, into our field we will find the deeply hidden needs of the soil there.

My grandfather's experienced hands and eyes were able to sense the condition of the soil he worked. He could detect the factors that nourished it and those that polluted it. He understood that over-farming without replenishing would rob the soil of the nutrients necessary for healthy plant. He internalized the need to cultivate, till, and care for the soil year after year and not give in to the larger atmosphere that threatened it. Grandpa knew that there were industrial farmers harvesting more than was necessary and selling out at a lower price, but he wanted the vegetables from his garden to be wholesome.

And so it is with us teachers in our environments, whatever those environments might be. God calls us to bear fruit in all that we do. In John 15:2 Jesus tells us that, like the branch of the fruit tree or the vine in the vineyard, anyone who doesn't bear fruit will be cut off. He also reminds us in John 15:16 that we have not chosen him but that he has chosen us, so that "you might go and bear fruit." It is our job to bear fruit. It is our reaction to the love of Christ that allows us to grow. As teachers, we in turn work for the growth of our students. In an effort to bear fruit we develop watchful eyes, gentle hands, and listening hearts. We know that history has in many cases polluted our field. We know that educational over-farming exists in initiatives aimed at increasing educational output with little regard for the long-term viability of students. We know that this activity depletes the environment for our students. We know that we must turn over the soil in our teaching environments and care deeply for our students so that the atmosphere in which we teach will be nourishing for our learners.

The environment in which any particular individual teaches may require more or less work in order for growth to occur. In discussing this with a variety of educators, I learned much about their perspectives on the current educational field. They shared their thoughts and ideas about the educational environment and what they experience there.

Like these teachers, Christ taught each day to crowds of people who came to learn from him. And like teachers who seek a purpose deeper than the written details of their curriculum, Jesus taught far beyond the written words in the Old Testament law. Because of this he found himself watched closely by the "experts in the law." They were the keepers of the minutiae of the written word and they wanted to see to it that Jesus held to their expectations. They challenged him, waiting for him to either give a wrong answer or to react wrongly to their challenges. They waited expectantly to try and see him stumble so that they could discredit him and his purposes. As you remember, these Pharisees were experts in the letter of the law. They placed value in the knowledge of the law and its exact application in life. What their focus neglected, though, was a deeper understanding of the meaning behind that law. Christ, on the other hand, understood the deep meaning of the law in his heart. His desire was for the growth of the people. He understood the field around him, and in that very field he worked his garden to produce fruit.

The parable of the Samaritan in Luke 10:25–37 shows us a good example of this. A law expert challenged Jesus' stance on eternal life and who would earn it. In this well-known story Jesus points out his understanding of political and social factions of the day as well as his disinterest in them. He looks past the intent of the critical listeners, allowing them to concentrate on their concerns while he drove toward the main point, which must be our main point as well: love your neighbor. This is a tiny little nugget of gold, "Love your neighbor." The love that Jesus suggested is the very love that so many miss, even Christians. This is the love of those who appear outside of your circle, beyond your radar screen, and often those who appear to stand in direct opposition to you. Christ's telling of this parable teaches us in our Christian walk as teachers. Its context also speaks to us about what we may encounter as we walk our calling in the field of education.

Its focus on love of neighbor instructs; its point makes itself clear, but the context in which the parable is told holds a lesson for us as well. Jesus taught many of the same lessons as the other teachers of his day. He spoke about the law. He drew its application into the lives of his listeners. He held up God's holiness as the standard. He understood the mindset behind what was being taught around him. He knew the emphasis placed on the details of the law, on the appearances of knowledge, on outward application. But Jesus knew what was missing in the teaching, and he brought that to his listeners.

In understanding our field we must recognize its contours. Just as Christ tracked with the Pharisees' standards of excellence, we agree with the standards of our profession. We see the necessary emphasis on information-based knowledge. This type of knowledge is important. It is also measurable, which makes it useful to those who assess the value of various types of knowledge. We sense the value of observable achievement and we agree with the significance of achievement. We also encourage the God-given curiosity and creativity that exists in teaching and learning. However, just as

Christ looked more deeply into the heart of teaching concerning the kingdom of God, he calls us to do so in our teaching. So while we celebrate the beneficial aspects of our teaching profession, we do so asking God to use us in it as faith-driven Christians.

And this is where our faith as Christians ties into our understanding of the field of teaching and learning. It is where Christ joined the teaching of his time. It is where we join the teaching of our time. More than sharing knowledge of facts and cognitive processes, we answer Christ's calling to live out the purpose behind knowledge. We do this through the manner in which we go about our work—in the joy we express through it. It is the difference between the intellectual farmer and the heart farmer. The intellectual farmer focuses on taking his tools to the garden and planting his garden according to the farmer's rulebook and the information in the seed pack. The heart farmer labors in the soil, understands its origin, and the meaning behind proper care of that soil. My grandfather was a heart farmer, and in turn his garden always produced more that was needed, allowing him to give away to others in need. And each season began with him walking around looking at the soil.

Reflect and discuss:

9. *How can we as teachers take a detailed walk around our field each season to gain a deeper feel for what it holds?*

10. *What are some Scripture verses/stories to hold in mind as we remind ourselves of the importance of teaching as Christ?*

3

The Soil

I REMEMBER ONE PARTICULAR spring when the Saturday work in the greenhouse seemed to take days rather than hours. Grandpa's methodic way of preparing the seeds and soil appeared so effortless and natural. Each stage had a purpose. He moved from one step to the next with finesse as though he really enjoyed the work, but for me it lacked variety and interest. I honestly couldn't decide whether I wanted to play in the dirt, so the time would go more quickly, or just race to get the work done . . . so I did a little of each. To save time and steps, I grabbed a scoop of dirt from the bag under the table and tossed it into the plastic tray where I was to sow the initial seed. I quickly spread the seed on the dirt, sprinkled water over it and snuck to the back of the greenhouse where the freshly planted trays were kept for germination. As I restarted the process on tray number two, Grandpa walked up behind me and placed the first tray in front of me. "Someone planted this one wrong," he gruffed. "They forgot to use the warmed dirt and fertilizer from the heater before seeding. I need you to replant it for me."

There was no questioning who that someone was; we were the only two in the greenhouse. So, with my tail between my legs, I walked outside and dumped the tray of dirt onto the compost pile behind the greenhouse, knowing that I had wasted seed and dirt with no benefit of time saved. I then rinsed out the tray and reloaded it with the right dirt, the dirt that Grandpa had pre-warmed on his self-built greenhouse heater. I scooped the prescribed amount of dung and potash and mixed it in. Finally, with the soil leveled, the tray was ready for seed.

"Grandpa," I asked sheepishly, "why are you so picky about the dirt in the trays?" Without stopping his work, he stated, "These seeds are tough. They'll grow in cold soil, but if we prepare the soil and give the seeds a warm place to be, with some good food and vitamins, they will grow better." Holding a seed in his hand, as if to make a point, he nodded, "A little bit of extra work at the start gives you stronger plants and better beans," which answered my other question about what we were planting that day.

My question must have hit a nerve with Grandpa, because he went on to explain the big plastic tank on the larger tractor. He told me how the soil is different from one end of the garden to the other and that it changes each year. He explained that we need to know each plot of earth so that we can add the right kind of fertilizer to help the plants grow, regardless of where they are. "We do the same thing here." Grandpa smiled, "If you want this seed to give you good food, you've got to take care of the ground. You don't just grab a bag of dirt and plant seed in it. You need to know what's in your dirt."

Then he went outside to the compost pile, where I had thrown the seeded dirt a few minutes earlier. When he returned, he held out his two hands with dirt in each. "Which dirt is going to give you a better plant?" he asked. When I told him that I didn't know, he told me to look more closely at the dirt in his hands. When I looked more closely, I could see that the color was a little different, but that I couldn't tell. He looked into my face and said, "Exactly! You can't just see it with your eyes. Sometimes you have to hold it." And he placed the dirt in my two hands. "Rub it between your fingers. What do you feel?" What I felt was grainy, airy soil in one hand and muddy, packed soil in the other. Then Grandpa told me to smell the dirt. When I did, I could smell two different smells. "Healthy soil smells and feels different from unhealthy soil," he said. "You can't always see it. Sometimes you have to feel it and smell it. If you know what soil you have, you can find out what it needs." And we went back to work—point made!

In the last chapter we talked about how important it is to understand the larger field in which we work, the field of education. We spoke about it in a global, professional sense. We learned about its past and how that past affects the present state of the field. But what about the soil in the field? What about the very matter into which teachers plant the seed? How do we understand it? How do we to come to know it and care for its needs? How do we understand its nature? Fortunately for us, the Bible offers plenty wisdom to help us along.

In Matthew 13:1–23 we find the well-known parable of the sower. Jesus tells his disciples about a farmer who goes out and sows seed. It is unclear exactly how it happens this way, but the seed lands on all different types of ground. With each type of soil comes a different result. Jesus wants his disciples to understand that good spiritual soil produces good fruit. He is speaking to his followers about the condition of their hearts as they hear his teaching. He uses a farming metaphor because the people who followed him were close to the earth and would understand it.

This farming metaphor applies to us as well. As Christian teachers we can understand the soil metaphor on multiple levels. One has to do with our own hearts. We will speak more about that in chapter 6. The more immediate application here is to recognize the soil in which we are planting the seeds of learning. Our contracted job is to plant the seed of content knowledge in our subject area. There is no mistake here. Our other role as Christians is to study and understand the soil into which we are planting that seed. It has needs that we must address, if the seed we plant there is going to take root and grow. The soil's needs change as seasons unfold and years pass, and we need to pay attention to that as well. The healthier the soil, the better chance the seed has to take root and grow.

As Jesus shared this parable, he also taught us about its application through both the explanation that he gave his disciples and through his deep understanding of the crowd that followed him to listen. The crowd that day was extremely large. By the time he reached the lake, he had to climb into a boat and push out from the shore so his listeners could fill in along the water's edge. We read that among his listeners that day were a demon-possessed man and some Pharisees. His crowd consisted of a variety of people, all types of soil. The Gospels show Jesus caring for the lepers, dining with the detested tax collectors, prostitutes, thieves, drunks, murderers . . . the list goes on. We also read that the blind and lame sought him out looking to be healed. Jesus' followers were the rocky ground, the thorny areas, the path, and the deep, rich soil. Knowing this, he intentionally spoke in parables, stories that carried embedded lessons. Some listeners only grasped the story at its surface, but they enjoyed it nonetheless, benefitting to the extent they were capable. Depending upon the soil represented by each listener, the parable delivered its meaning.

If we read ourselves into this account in Matthew 13, if we place ourselves into the sharing of the parable, we can easily see our roles as teachers being similar to the job of the sower, the farmer. Picture the farmer as he walked across his field, carrying a sack of seed with him. He reached into that sack over and over, drawing out handfuls of seed and casting it out onto the soil. The seed that the farmer cast onto the field was small and didn't weigh much. And so, until it reached the soil and become damp, it could easily be blown around by the slightest breeze. The farmer took a chance each time he reached out his hand to spread more seed. He couldn't always determine where it would land or how it would grow, but he sowed anyway, knowing that his care of the soil would give his seed the best opportunity of taking root and producing fruit. He also knew that the seed that did take root would produce two things: fruit to feed, and more seed for sowing.

This is the case with teachers as well. The seed that we sow is of two natures. One is the seed of knowledge that we disseminate (spread seed) to our students. The other is the spiritual seed that Jesus tells us to always spread though our way of living—how we speak, how we act and react, how we listen, and how we think. Like the farmer, however, we aren't always aware of where the seed will land or what the nature of the soil is. We sow the seed, though, praying that it will take root and produce. As we consider this, it makes sense to remember the farmer's lessons and learn what we can about the soil in which we scatter seeds, so that we can care for and build up that soil. How mature is it? What matter does it contain? How can we build its nutrients? How do we measure its health?

Reflect and discuss:

11. *Brainstorm and discuss some practical ways that we can look at the soil of a classroom to understand its content?*

12. *How can the students be directly involved?*

13. *How can it be done indirectly?*

In Christianity we often speak about children in the faith. We hold a measuring stick that the Bible gives us, and sometimes use reference to milk versus solid food like Paul did in 1 Corinthians 3:2. He said that the believers at Corinth received milk from him and not solid food, because they were not ready for it. Perhaps Paul was indicating that they were shallow soil, not giving depth for roots. This sort of terminology can be useful when talking about believers within the church, but we are speaking about the world in general. And so we need to use terms that are more in line with the world's measuring stick. For that reason I would like to use some terms from renowned developmental psychologist Erik Erikson. Erikson observed human life throughout his time teaching and studying psychology. His picture of a person's psychosocial development spanned from birth to death and divided a lifespan into eight stages. By the time children enter school, they have passed through three of Erikson's stages and fit roughly into two of the others in his theory.

Each stage comes at a given point in life as the result of a person's psychosocial environment and growth. In order for a person to grow into a psychologically healthy person, normal development must take place from one stage to another. Erikson believed that each stage is represented by a specific type of conflict, and the positive or negative outcome of that conflict either enhances or interferes with the person's further psychological development. It either helps or impairs the person's self-concept.

ELEMENTARY SCHOOL

As earlier stated, by the time children first reach elementary school they have seen the first three of Erikson's stages. They have worked through the issue of trust versus mistrust during their first eighteen months of life. The following year and a half has taught them about autonomy over and against shame and doubt. Ages three through six instruct them in the matter of initiative versus guilt. How these children experience life when we first see them depends heavily on the support that they have received from their families, friends, and other caretakers during these first three stages.

In elementary school children experience a need to succeed and master basic skills necessary in life and society. They are in what Erikson calls the latency stage, which spans approximately from age six to age twelve. In this stage children begin to acquire fundamental knowledge, and they start learning about what it means to take pride in their work. They want to do well, and we as teachers need to understand this and encourage them. During this stage children are learning to follow rules and respect them. They learn about cooperative work and play. This is also where they learn to recognize the various roles of people, individuals' behavior, and others' feelings. They build a strong connection between what they can achieve and who they are. During this stage children develop their first sense of competence. A child who succeeds here will likely develop a strong sense of usefulness and industry. The opposite is true for the child who doesn't succeed. Hence the deep importance of positive connection and relationship building between elementary school teachers and their students.

MIDDLE SCHOOL AND HIGH SCHOOL

Erikson names the next stage of development adolescence, which is convenient for us to remember because it corresponds exactly with how we refer to middle school– and high school–aged children. The conflict for this stage is one that requires particular attention on our part as teachers because of the implications for the rest of life. In Erikson's theory the conflict of adolescence is that of identity versus identity confusion. During the period of life spanning from approximately ages twelve to eighteen, students are consciously or subconsciously working out three major questions: "Where do I come from?," "Who am I?," and "What do I want to become?" These questions represent a person's search for a synthesis of the past, the present, and the future; in other words, a search for unity.

In past generations, where the community and the family provided role models for children, these questions were easier to answer. Children were able to more easily understand their context and establish their identity. This is no longer a foregone conclusion. Society and family do not necessarily share the same goals. Older generations often fail at providing appropriate role models for younger people. Furthermore, the rapid shift of societal mores can cause a lack in personal stability. This leaves teens looking for a reflection of themselves in others' eyes to begin building a self-image. They seek identity more within their peer groups and social media contact and less within the family. They look for assuredness and recognition from the people around them "who count." At this stage kids are especially looking for fidelity, for someone they can trust and to whom they can be true. This is where a sense of commitment begins.

It is important to understand the outcomes of this stage on both the positive and negative side. The person who succeeds in the challenges of adolescence will be the one who finds and establishes continuity between the past, the present, and the future. This person will have found positive answers to the questions about origin, person, and future direction. As a result, this person will have established some solidity in value system (religious beliefs), vocational goals, life philosophy, and sexuality. Conversely, possible outcomes are role confusion in life, self-doubt, and possibly a self-destructive, one-sided preoccupation with self. Moreover, this person will potentially spend a great deal of his or her life either worried about the opinions of others, at one extreme, or floundering in addiction, at the other.

So, with an understanding of these two stages, how do we know where to scatter seed? Remember the parable of the sower. Some landed on the path and was trampled. Some landed on the thorny ground and was choked out. Some landed on the rocky ground with thin soil and sprang up quickly, but because of its shallow soil it died in the heat of the sun. Still other seed landed in rich soil and took root. The parable seems clear that the sower scattered seed. He didn't appear to draw lines along which he scattered it. He merely scattered the seed. Christ did the same. As he told his parables and healed, the sound of his voice went out to all—the seekers, the believers, the skeptics, the lost, and the Pharisees. Jesus spoke honestly, healed people openly, and lived what he preached in front of everyone. Seed was not spared; there was sufficient water and plenty of the sun. Those who were ready to receive what he shared did; those who were not did not. In teaching, we understand that the kids in our classrooms can potentially represent any combination of soil types. We do not always have a clear picture of the soil during each hour of each day, but that should not keep us from taking time to study the "soil samples" that our students represent and make efforts to help them grow.

SOIL SAMPLES

Over the course of years spent with learners, we realize that certain students stand out in their memories. Sometimes this comes as a result of specific conversations with a student or the trials connected with that young person. Often it is connected to an individual's life circumstances that tug at the teacher's heart. These and all the other kids make up the soil into which we sow seed as teachers. The samples below include a spectrum of students. Some of them represent students I have come to know personally; others are stories that I have been able to gather from teachers who have shared with me. Reflecting on each case though has taught me a great deal, not only about how to walk alongside of and teach my students, but about young people in general. In some cases I learned about the blessings that some teachers have been in the lives of their students. In other cases I reached a deeper understanding of the blessing that our profession offers through the lives of the students with whom we work and the value involved in a teacher who seeks to understand the students that surround him or her. In all cases I was reminded of the precious people we encounter as teachers, the eternal implications of our interactions with them, and the necessity of understanding what we can about who they are. Let's look together at some of these kids . . . let's dig!

Amy, a high school senior in the Midwest, appears to be as settled as any other girl her age. She carries around her smart phone, texts with her friends, and has her own car. If you were to observe Amy in her daily setting, you would see a young woman who has it all together. She looks self-assured and strong. What doesn't appear on the surface is her family struggle. Amy's parents were divorced when she was five, and Amy hasn't seen her father (by his choice) since she was in seventh grade. At one point her father submitted an official statement to the court that he wanted no contact with his daughters. While Amy was in junior high school her mother was diagnosed with a mental disorder. The challenges coming from that disorder have impacted Amy heavily. When Amy had been younger, her mother had been heavily involved in the lives of Amy's older siblings. As Amy approached her teens, however, that same mother suddenly refused to participate in her daughter's school and social life. Amy once asked her mother about this. Her mother simply told her that boys and girls are different; that Amy's brothers needed her but Amy doesn't. Despite Amy's protest, the case was closed, as far as Amy's mother was concerned.

Amy works because she wants to work, but also because she must. She pays for her own clothes, her car, her phone, and gas. She also regularly gives money to her mom to help keep family finances afloat. Amy's mother works, but her earnings, even when combined with social assistance, sometimes come up short. Amy despises this. She disagrees with the entire situation. She rejects the fact that she and her sister receive free-and-reduced breakfast and lunch at school. In her mind, everyone should contribute what they can to the system to help others, even she and her family. Her consolation is in the understanding and belief that life will not always be like this for her. She intends to work her way out of it.

John, a recent college graduate, grew up in a church-going family. His parents divorced when he was in the sixth grade. John has good relationships with both of his parents, but he struggles with self-concept. He is receptive and hard working, but shy. John worked very hard in school, but had no idea what he was supposed to study in college. He was constantly searching, like many students his age, though he didn't know what he was searching for. He didn't know what his gifts were, nor did he really know if he had any talents. John appeared to be the quintessential nice guy. Underneath he was full of questions about where he came from, who he was, and where he was going. He couldn't understand why his parents divorced, especially since his dad constantly regretted the fact. What John really wanted the most were answers, even if he couldn't articulate the questions while he was in school.

John's upbringing held some paradox. Before his parents divorced, the family attended church together each week. John could remember the heavy-handed teaching of the pastor and had a hard time wanting to believe. He felt that the pastor's portrayal of God made it almost impossible to succeed in getting into heaven. He wanted to have faith, but the model that had be given to him taught him that it would be a harsh journey. As a result, John continued attending church with his father because he felt that it was the right thing to do, but John's faith was more duty-bound than relational.

Kelly is a girl who comes from a large family with several siblings. She works hard in school and wants to please her teachers. Being in the middle of the group of siblings, she wrestles with who she is: the younger sister, the older sister, the next in command after mom, etc. Kelly sees older brothers who are, in her opinion, able to do as they please and younger siblings whom she feels aren't responsible enough. She holds many responsibilities: cooking, cleaning, laundry, and some discipline of younger siblings. Wanting to have some additional direction, she frequently asks teachers' opinions and is more than willing to share her troubles with her classmates. Because of her large family and the connected responsibilities, she often carries the role she plays among her younger siblings into the classroom. As a result Kelly appears to be the mother hen in class interactions and among her friends. Kelly's family is intact with excellent communication. Her mother is strong in her faith, and her father is a solid spiritual leader. The family worships together weekly and is heavily involved in a faith community. They work out all problems at the dinner table. Kelly regularly challenges her mother's authority, though. She feels that the rules are unreasonable, and she regularly looks for input from others to support her stance. She feels she is right, and she invests great effort to prove herself.

Joel is a sophomore who brings juggling balls to school. His favorite activity is juggling. Joel is non-confrontational, but participates little. He does not do his homework and does not give excuses. If you were to ask Joel for an explanation, he would shrug his shoulders and make a face of chagrin. Joel does not think school is fun. Homework is even less fun. In fact, he cannot see any point to any of it. He can see no connection between school and his future, and so he experiences no imperative in trying.

One day Joel's teacher sat down for lunch with Joel, a student with consistently low grades in that class. He wanted to talk with him about school and how he was feeling about the year. He acknowledged that school was not hard. Confused about how easy classes translated into his low quiz and test scores, he dug a bit deeper and asked about Joel's home life. When the teacher asked him about whether his parents would help him with his homework, he began to relate his story. His mother had a successful career that required her to work long hours and return home late. Dad was home most evenings, but his time was spent mostly in front of the television or working at the computer. When the teacher asked Joel about what his parents thought about his interest in juggling, he explained that his parents didn't think that he would go anywhere with juggling. The one thing that brings him joy is the very activity that they reject. This thought pricked his teacher's heart, and the teacher mentioned a clowning troupe about which he knew. When he suggested to Joel that this clowning troupe was in the area, and that its members liked to welcome new people who are interested, his eyes began to light up. He proudly informed the teacher that some clowns juggle, and he wanted to know how he could make contact. Interestingly enough, when the teacher stopped the conversation to find the email address of the clown troupe, Joel's demeanor changed from one of moderate disinterest to one of full attention, not only in the conversation, but also in class.

Jenny is a quiet, energetic young lady with a soft and sweet demeanor. Her searching eyes are bright. Jenny stays close to her friends. She is comfortable when she is around people she knows and trusts. She will speak to new faces, but carefully. As I came to know Jenny and meet her parents, I learned that her mother had been fighting terminal cancer with an unforeseeable timeline. Jenny's father, a pastor of a small country church, was doing his best to faithfully lift up his family and community. Jenny's mother attends all conferences and openly reaches out to teachers in Christian love.

When Jenny sits in class, she seems to have a private secret that she would like to share with everyone, if she only had the courage to do so. She smiles and nods at the irony of many situations that elude most kids in the classroom. She understands more than she allows others to know. Outside class, Jenny participates in her youth group and leads a small group in her church's children's ministry program. She runs cross-country and enjoys laughing with friends. When asked about her mother's struggle with cancer, she told me that she doesn't always know how to think about it. Sometimes she really breaks down and asks God why this is happening, but when she comes around to listening to him she understands in her heart that he made her mother. Jenny explained to me that he gets to decide when he will bring her home, and when that happens he will give her and her father the strength to work through the pain and loss.

Then there is Elliot. Elliot is a one of two identical twins, the oldest of their mother's children. They have one sister and two half-siblings. Elliot and his brother were born when their mother was in her early high school years, and their sister was born two years later. Because their mom was too young to raise the children on her own, Elliot and his siblings lived together with their mother and grandfather during their early years. Their father seldom made contact; he didn't want to be "tied down with kids."

After a few years, Elliot's mother met another man who was also young. He had been in some trouble with minor misdemeanors and was driving on a limited license. His looks bore a strong resemblance to Elliot's father, and the two of them soon moved in together. They are the parents of Elliot's two youngest half-siblings. For the last seven years they have lived in a rented house on a busy road. Their mother loves the children deeply, and the children know it. She works extremely long hours to try and provide what she can. Because of a lack of education, she has nearly reached her low professional ceiling. When possible, she tries to take a class to change that, but life is busy with five children at home. Her former live-in boyfriend and the father of two of the children was unable to work because of his suspended driver's license. From time to time an acquaintance would hire him to do under-the-table work hanging vinyl siding or tearing off a roof, but that work was inconsistent at best.

Elliot prefers being at school and friends' houses to spending time at home. His reasons for this are many. When his mother's boyfriend invited friends to their house there was a lot of drinking, and the friends were rough. They swore and watched inappropriate films around the younger children. The birthday tradition for this boyfriend was to give the boys a birthday punch in the stomach to "teach him to be a man." This boyfriend no longer lives with the family, nor does he have any contact with his own children. The mom has since moved on to another companion.

Elliot therefore tries to go to friends' houses as often as possible on the weekends and during vacations. He has one friend whose family has taken him in and become very close to Elliot. They invite him to their house as often as possible. Typically, a Friday overnight stay will stretch into Sunday, which Elliot enjoys. This family has grown deeply in their church community, and Elliot has become a regular face in that community. He looks forward to Wednesday nights when he goes to his friend's house for dinner and then to youth group.

These students are a sample of the many whose stories I have been fortunate enough to share directly, observe at a distance, or encounter through interviews, as they make their daily journey through life and school. They are not a full representation of the population that fills our classrooms and hallways on a daily basis.

There are some struggles that these students share with all of their peers. Each of these young people walks though life, growing, and asking questions about their past, present, and future. They want to establish their identity where they are, and they look at their peers, their parents, and other figures in their environment to help them. Some of these kids come out of solid homes led by parents who understand, or at least seek to understand, their children. These parents engage their children and listen to them. They guide them and support them. Other parents are absent, either physically or emotionally. Intentionally or unintentionally they leave their children to navigate life on their own. You can doubtless add to this list a number of similar or even more severe scenarios in which kids come to your classes wondering what will come next, who they are, and how they have reached a particular point in life. They make up the soil of a teacher's garden, the very garden into which we scatter seed each day.

Reflect and discuss:

14. What stories can you share about the students you have encountered? Where have you been pleased, surprised, heartbroken? Which soil-type does each represent?

15. How could your story affect the kind of soil you are today? How
could that story enrich that of your students?

NUMBERS IN THE SOIL

One verse that we often refer to in raising and teaching children is found in Proverbs 22:6, "Start children off on the way they should go, and even when they are old they will not turn from it." We hear pastors preach sermons on its wisdom. We read chapters devoted to it in Christian parenting books, and we pray that parents and guardians hear the message and take it to heart. Regardless of the parental response to Proverb's calling, there is more at play in the life of a child than just the influences at home. Parents are statistically the first and most important factor influencing the decisions that children make, but there are other factors that cannot be ignored. These factors affect the soil of the garden in which we work. It concerns time: the amount of time children spend in the presence of their parents daily from birth until they begin school, how much time they then spend with their parents while they are students, and how many hours per week and per year they are under the influence of others.

A 2014 American Time Use Survey conducted by the U.S. Bureau of Labor and reports,

> Adults living in households with children under age 6 spent an average of 2.0 hours per day providing primary childcare to household children. Adults living in households where the youngest child was between the ages of 6 and 17 spends less than half as much time providing primary childcare to household children—49 minutes per day. Primary childcare is childcare that is done as a main activity, such as providing physical care or reading to children.[1]

These numbers drop with the increase of education and employment. Sharing these statistics is not intended to indicate an increase or decrease trend in child-parent time, nor are they intended to place any level of onus on parents, but merely to give a point of reference for our comparison.

---

1 U.S. Department of Labor, "American Time Use Survey Summary."

Once children begin school, around age six, they spend roughly seven hours per day in school. In elementary school these hours are spent primarily in the presence of one classroom teacher. That teacher carries the responsibility of shaping the children's picture of learning and creating for up to thirty-five hours each week during nine months out of the year. The teacher receives the children in school when they are fresh from bed and returns them to their parents after a long day of work, learning, growing, and creating. The teacher shares a great deal of life with children, discussing the world, exploring the children's hopes and fears, beliefs, and desires. During this time children grow and develop under the tutelage of many teachers, who hold a considerable amount of responsibility for the molding of minds. The teacher's hopes, dreams, thoughts, and fears can be easily transferred and become the children's hopes, dreams, thoughts, and fears as a class spends long hours on the journey of learning.

As these same kids move to middle school and high school, the amount of time spent in connection with school often increases with a host of school-related activities that are frequently supported and directed by the same teachers that the students see in class. Through the multiple levels of involvement that kids maintain with the school community, they begin to develop an additional layer of identity that is interwoven with that community. Its thoughts can easily become their thoughts. Its leaders become role models for them and the soil becomes altered.

Considering all of this information in layers, I'm forced back to that greenhouse. I'm forced to consider the bags of soil and the nutrients that went into it, the attention that my grandfather paid to ensure just the right mixture for the best possible root growth. Grandpa wanted to be certain that each plant could grow as much as possible and become as strong as it could before we transplanted it into the less protected environment of the garden. It all started with the soil . . . before the seed could be planted. Grandpa was a master at reading the soil. He could feel it. He could smell it. He understood it. Then, through wisdom and experience, he knew what to do with it. How will we come to know the soil into which we are called to plant seed? What will we do to build the soil?

Apply:

Let's take the questions at the end of the paragraph above and apply them to our own situations. The first question revisits an earlier matter, but the second draws us a step further and points us to our next chapter.

16. *How does the steady increase of peer group influence play a role here?*

17. *How can a responsibility to build the soil be blended into the academic responsibilities of the teacher?*

4

The Place of the Farmer

GRANDPA SPENT AN IMMENSE amount of time working the soil. From early February, when he first began setting up the greenhouses, all the way through late autumn, when the last of the harvest was brought in, Grandpa worked in the dirt. Some people said that they could even smell the soil on him when they sat next to him at Sunday dinner. I used to laugh at that—until I spent my first full season working with my grandpa, rather than just working when I wanted money. There are some notable things that happen after you work in a garden for a longer period of time. One of them is that your hands begin to change. They become stronger as a result of your work digging, hoeing, picking vegetables, and carrying water hoses. Another is that you begin to associate yourself more with your work and start thinking more about things like the weather and where the sun is in the sky. A third thing that happens is that you become more aware of the purpose behind what you are doing and what needs to be done. You slowly realize that you are doing more than working in a garden.

One hot August morning, my grandfather gave my cousin and me the job of filling a wagonload of tomato boxes. The vegetable stand that Grandma ran had been booming with customers wanting tomatoes, and Grandpa didn't want anyone to be disappointed. "I have to run to the bank and go to the grocery store for your grandma," Grandpa informed us, "and I want the two of you to fill every one of these boxes this morning. When I get back, I'll help you finish, and we'll bring them up for her. It'll be busy this afternoon. People will want to start canning, and they need tomatoes."

I'm not sure how much contact you have had with middle school–age boys, but apparently Grandpa had more faith in us than we had in ourselves. Within a few minutes of his departure the first half-rotten tomato landed on my foot. There was no way I could let that happen and ignore it. It was a matter of pride, or so I reasoned. So, after I had looked over my shoulder to see where my cousin was, I gripped a juicy tomato in my hand, wheeled around, and let it loose. It was a direct hit. Juice and seeds ran down the side of his head, and I quickly learned something about my cousin's passion to win a fight. After what seemed like an entire morning of tomato pitching, we noticed that we had only partially filled our first boxes. We decided to get to call it a truce and work. We both hoped our grandfather wouldn't be too angry. By the time Grandpa returned we had only half-filled the wagon with tomatoes. What's more, there was no way of hiding what we had done with the rest of our time. Grandpa looked at our clothes and the evidence littering the ground. He sent my cousin to the bean patch to begin picking there and gave me a new tomato box to begin filling. He assigned me to a row next to him and said, "We're behind, and people will be here later for their tomatoes. Let's pick."

I'm not certain what hit me more, Grandpa's lack of outward emotion toward what my cousin and I had done, or his sense of purpose in moving forward. As the two of us picked that day, he began to hum the chorus of an old hymn I knew. I kept sneaking peeks at him to see his expression at the mess, but there was none. The wrinkles in his neck spoke to me though. They were the wrinkles of years spent doing something my grandfather believed in. The massive size of his hands likewise came from his using them to accomplish a goal worth reaching, and being there with him taught me that our time in the garden was more than a list of tasks to accomplish. Moreover, his quiet non-response to the tomato fight that my cousin and I had had taught me that maybe he wasn't angry. Perhaps he understood us better than we thought. Maybe he knew that we needed to have fun in the middle of the work, because it is all part of the journey.

Some years later, when my grandpa had passed away I began to reflect more on that first full season of work in the garden, I started to understand that our work there was bigger than merely preparing the soil, planting the seed, and harvesting it. I began to look into the process of keeping the garden. I realized that when you invest your time and energy there, raising the plants, removing weeds, feeding and watering the soil, you begin to see your work less as a list of tasks and more as a journey to a purpose. You spend time listening to the wind, checking the temperature, watching the clouds. You do this because you understand, sometimes at a very subconscious level, that you are not just taking part in the production of food; you are participating in a plan given to you by God. You grasp that the plan is to bear fruit that will feed others. The hours of time spent together with my grandfather instructed me. There was some talking and much work. We rode the tractors together and planted the vegetables together, according to his careful instruction. We placed straw around the tomatoes in a certain way, and when the watermelon was ripe we enjoyed a fresh slice right from the garden. All of those hours of work, all of the watching and following, taught me important lessons about life. Some of them were apparent then, while most became clear later; but all of them were learned while working alongside a master gardener.

When we read the various Gospel accounts, we learn much through Christ's time with his disciples. They spent many hours together, walking through fields, along the sea, across rivers, and near groves. The disciples followed Jesus and watched as he spoke, taught, healed, and pointed out life to them. In the midst of all the teaching that Christ did, much of his time was spent showing the disciples what they already had in them and then taught them how to see it through a new set of eyes, eternal eyes. He often spoke to them in everyday agricultural terminology. He used metaphors and parables from their life and time and then gave them a deeper look into the truth that life communicated through very simple yet very profound realities. They were serious together. They laughed together. They worked together. They were on a powerful journey together. The sheer amount of time that the disciples spent in Jesus' presence connected them to him at a deep level. Jesus' many roles spoke to their needs. He was their teacher, their shepherd, a master fisherman, a healer, a planter, and a revolutionary. The manner in which Jesus saw life was different from how the disciples had learned to see it in their homes. The way in which Jesus spoke and acted was unique. Everything about him was different, and this drew the disciples to be with him on his journey.

If we take these thoughts with us into the classroom, we don't need to stretch to see the many connections. It would be bold and arrogant to equate ourselves as teachers with Jesus. Nonetheless, there are some undeniable relationships between his work and the work we are called to do in our position as teachers. As we saw in the last chapter, we too spend large amounts of time with students. We invite young people on a learning journey, one that is practical, academic, and at times emotional. We work with them to help them see life from a new and more profound perspective, and that work takes place at the exact time in their lives where they are asking the questions that we discussed in the last chapter: where they come from, why they are here, what they should be doing, and where they are going. This plays psychologically on the minds of the learners. Learning and thinking about life through various sets of eyes triggers their hopes and passions, worldviews and opinions. The way in which we speak and listen, how we act, and how we live all transmit our view of the world to the kids around us. Without necessarily using any specific words, we project a worldview through our teaching. Which worldview we are reflecting, though, depends on how we live, speak, listen, and act.

Reflect and discuss:

In considering how we project our worldview, consider the following questions and discuss them:

18. *What examples of teachers from your past can you share to illustrate worldview projection via how that person/those people live, speak, listen, and act?*

19. *How/why is it important to maintain a strong consciousness of the connection between our outward living and what it reflects of us and God?*

20. *What about your mannerisms and words transmit your what you hold to be true and sacred? What do they say?*

These ideas never really occurred to me early in my teaching career. I can no longer remember what kept me from making the connection, but I didn't. I remember regularly asking God why he had made me a teacher and then waiting for an answer. The answer never came in the form of words, but always through people. Generally it was an unexpected student or group of students (kids whom I didn't believe I was reaching) needing extra help in my class or wanting advice about something. Other times I heard my answer in an unexpected coffeehouse conversation with a parent wanting to talk with me about his or her student. Sometimes the conversation with parents would meander into the topic of worldview and faith.

As time passed, God opened my mind and heart to see where he was moving, or rather how he was moving me. Little by little, the Holy Spirit began to open my eyes to my purpose as a teacher and how it was tied into him. Moreover, he gave me more clarity about the deep responsibility of that calling.

Each time I stand in a classroom, each class, there is a new group of students, and during that period each day we learn together for an hour or more. Day after day and through that learning we build community. We work to develop relationships built on trust, common interest, and common learning goals. Over the course of a semester, a year, sometimes four years, life happens. Each person in the class journeys through times of joy and sorrow, pain and recovery, frustration and relief. These emotions follow the students to class, become part of the conversation, and often find themselves integrated in the class learning because that is how community works. How I as the teacher act, listen, speak, and receive the kids in the midst of their journey speaks to them. It either builds community and relationship or breaks it down. In any case, it speaks to them about who I am and what I hold to be true. Ultimately, it either honors God or not.

Paul encapsulates some of this in Ephesians 4:29–32. His words remind us to

> not let any unwholesome talk come out of your mouths,
> but only what is helpful for building others up according

(handwritten margin note: If we are in community & relationship so how we act will affect him!)

to their needs, that it may benefit those who listen. And
do not grieve the Holy Spirit of God, with whom you
were sealed for the day of redemption. Get rid of all
bitterness, rage and anger, brawling and slander, along
with every form of malice. Be kind and compassionate to
one another, forgiving each other, just as in Christ God
forgave you.

He is telling the community of believers at Ephesus that the way
they speak and, by extension, how they live and respond, needs to
build others up, not tear them down. He reminds us that God has
placed eternity in our hearts. He wants us to act in love, not irrita-
tion, and kindness, not malice. This can be a tall order when we are
surrounded by young people trying to understand who they are.

At this point we need to remember that our place as teachers
is one with many varied roles, each of which is based on relationship—relationship with God and relationship with the kids who
refer to us as us their teacher. As we saw in the chapter on the
soil, each student in our class community carries a different past
and present, a different perspective of reality, and a different set of
needs. Some of the kids we teach come from supportive, involved
families. In these cases our job description is easy: share experience, convey knowledge and application, grow community, help
the students seek and find their roles within that community, and
encourage them. Some learners live lives filled with challenges and
questions. Others come to us each day in a fully engaged survival
mode. With them the range of our work may grow as we learn
about their needs. In all cases it is our task to learn what we can
about each student in our classes, listening, watching, and lifting
them up in the appropriate way. Some need very little, whereas
others need much more than we could ever offer. We cannot fix
kids; we can, however, care for them, build them up, guide them,
and point them in the right direction.

One day after school I sat in a local coffee shop, and Ethan,
a student whom I didn't know very well, walked in. He saw me
sitting in the corner and approached me with tears in his eyes. I
didn't notice the tears right away, because I had been working at

my computer when he asked if we could talk. As looked up from my computer, I saw an otherwise confident young man trampled down by something heavy. Ethan wanted to discuss a problem between himself and his girlfriend. He explained that she suddenly wouldn't talk to him, but only text. After listening to his entire story, it was apparent to me that their dating relationship was about to end, despite his confidence to the contrary. When I asked Ethan if he has spoken to his parents about the matter, he looked at me in a very sober manner and told me that his parents would never understand, an assumption often made by teenagers. He felt that they would think that he was being overly dramatic about the whole thing. I asked Ethan to tell me why he felt this way, and he unpacked a long story about his parents. He told me about how they react to his life and try to fix the mistakes that had been made on his brother by keeping from repeating them in Ethan's life. The result of his parents' error correction was that their son was now confiding in a teacher rather than them.

In contrast with Ethan, there is Matthew, a young man coming from a heavily supportive family with four children. Matthew walked up to me one day and handed me an envelope. When I asked him what it was, his response was, "I was wondering if you would have time to come to my hockey game this Friday night. There are two tickets here. Maybe you could bring your wife or your son. My parents wanted me to invite someone important." Matthew is the boy who gives his all to everything that he does. He needs to work harder than the average student, but he does what he needs to do. His family supports him in all he endeavors and teaches him to live a life of faith. They do this through their church involvement and through their example of hard work, clean living, and community involvement. Matthew isn't the first child from this family that has been one of my students. He is the fourth. Each of his brothers had equally solid character, a clear testimony of the family's commitment to their kids. His mother participates in the local Moms in Touch group, which prays for the school community and spoils the teachers with treats during conferences each year. Her desire is that her children's teachers would affirm the family teachings and values and join her and her husband in being strong models to their children.

If every student were blessed by the family situation that Matthew enjoys, our calling as teachers would be vastly different. If we could count on kids with a deep self-concept and understanding of who they are in their families and their communities, our role might be merely that of sharing knowledge and experience and re-affirming what the kids already understand about morals and ethics. Unfortunately, like weeds and pollution to a farmer, sin denies us that ease. Along with the kids who have been firmly established at home, we are blessed by the challenge of reaching out to those whose background is less rosy.

Liz is one such girl. She is a young lady who graduated several years ago and presented me quite a different type of student. A very intelligent girl, Liz first came to my acquaintance as a freshman in high school. Her favorite color was black, and she very much enjoyed medieval garb. Liz also read incessantly. Her hard work was only exceeded by her willingness to participate in class. She had a best friend, Sam, who was also in the class. Together they set a new bar of difficulty that hour each day. Their presence was one of unexpected blessing, for they succeeded in both challenging their classmates to work harder and causing me to pray for them on the way to school each day, asking God about how to help them. You see, both of these extremely bright kids came out of broken, abusive, and financially struggling homes, each with only one parent. Both of them expressed a desire to talk about all matters temporal and spiritual, and both of them wanted to do so during the school day. That was precisely the time when it was prohibited for me to discuss spiritual issues. Furthermore, they were both minors, and I made it clear to them that I could talk with them about such things outside of school with their parents' permission. They did not want that, because they felt that their parents wouldn't understand and would reject the idea.

How do we as Christian teachers live and teach in a way that recognizes the needs of each of these students and the many others that join them in class each day? How do we make time to listen to those who need a set of ears, offer advice to students whose parents are unavailable to help their sons and daughters navigate life? How do we sooth the pains of those whose homes are in shambles, or account for the fact that without the free breakfast and lunch programs at our school certain students in our classes would have only one meal each day? How do we hear the spiritual outcries of the searchers, knowing that in some cases we are legally bound to silence on certain matters?

An often-used quote attributed to Francis of Assisi speaks out of the past in this regard: "Preach the Gospel at all times, and if necessary use words."[1] These words hit home on a regular basis because of where I work. I want each of my students to see me living a life of joy and gratefulness. I want them to witness a clear consistency between what I believe and how I live. There should be no division between my worldview and my conduct. If I make a mistake, I must be ready to acknowledge it, and in doing so I need to be ready to extend grace to my students when they make mistakes. When I speak, my words should be "seasoned with salt," as Colossians 4:6 says. When I listen, I want to hear the words of James 1:19 and "be quick to listen, slow to speak and slow to become angry." I am fully aware that I cannot give my students a perfect model of Christ. What I do want to do, though, is live humbly before them, giving them a model of a person who is growing in the faith that he professes, regardless of how often he falls. I want them to encounter a person who does not create a division between the intellectual life and the faith life, but seeks harmony between them. In doing this I want to see each student's needs for what they are, lovingly attending to those that I can, and prayerfully lifting them up when their needs which are beyond my ability to help.

Certain students whom we teachers see each day may need nothing beyond our teaching than encouragement to follow in the path that their parents have already pointed out for them. They are rooted in stabile families that guide them and build them up in Christ. Kelly, whom we met in chapter 3, exemplifies this. She is

1. Carlson, *Who'll Be in Heaven & Who Won't?*, 100.

the girl from the large family whose parents gather the entire group of kids around the table for dinner each evening. Her mother and father have raised her with a strong sense of who she is, both in Christ and in the family. This young lady requires little more than encouragement and steadfastness. Her spiritual compass has been set, and the family and faith community work together to keep it pointed. As Kelly grows she will weather storms and have some leaves blown off of her branches, but, similarly to others like her, she is deeply rooted and hearty.

For each strong and hearty student, though, there are others who are very frail. They have received little support and need encouragement and guidance so that they can grow. Without support they will be easily emotionally trampled in hard times. Michael is one such student. He is fascinated by anything electronic, especially if it contains a computer processor. In class though, Michael tries to sit as far from the activity as possible. It seems as though he prefers to not be seen. Whenever he can, Michael will try to work alone, even if a class activity really requires interaction. Getting to know Michael was a challenge. At first he always spoke and listened with a down-tilted head, looking submissively over the tops of his glasses. His eyes dug into mine, looking for evidence that he could trust me. After many conversations I finally learned why. Michael had come from a home absent of a father figure. His mother always worked extremely hard to provide for family needs. This has left Michael alone on most afternoons and all summer. As a coping mechanism he learned to program computers quite well, and was part of several online gaming forums. Nothing in Michael's life had inspired him to grow. No one had stopped to notice that he was only growing at ground level. I sensed that God was letting me in on this and calling me to intervene. There was an opportunity more intentionality into how I interacted with Michael.

Not wanting to single out Michael and make him feel like a patient on a counselor's caseload, I decided to give him some space, while letting him know that he was important. Each day, as I stood at the door to greet the class, I began to shift my body language to draw his face upward to look at me when I said hello.

I began to ask him a different type of question about himself each day, and then build on that question the next day. Sometimes the questions were simply about his weekend. Other times I asked him a question about some computer application that I didn't understand very well. Slowly I began to ask about work and home. Over the course of two years (a long time indeed) Michael slowly opened up and began to trust me. Little changed about his comfort level with others around him, but he did change in some ways. Michael began smiling more. He started seeking me out when he needed help. Moreover, he slowly moved into a self-appointed role in the class. In looking at my class webpage, Michael decided it needed an upgrade. As a result he began monitoring my webpage. Scouring the page weekly, he informed me whenever he felt that something needed improvement. The most rewarding change in Michael came one morning before school. He cornered me in the hall to tell me some bad news. Michael looked me square in the eye and said, "I know that we're in school and everything, but something happened and I know that you go to church. Will you pray for . . . ?" and he told me the rest of the story, never waiting for my response to his request.

It came as a great surprise at first that Michael knew this about me, but after thinking about the matter for a while the mystery left. The community in which I work is not limited to the school in which I teach. It extends into the larger town in which I live, shop, dine out, worship, and sit down for a cup of coffee with friends. Since people in communities talk and pass information from one circle to the next, it should not have surprised me that Michael knew this about me. As a matter of fact, one day I shared this story with Shannon, a friend who teaches in another local school district. As my story continued, a smile grew on her face, and her head began to nod. It was clear that she wanted to relate to what she was hearing.

While co-teaching a course that included some special-needs students the previous year, this woman had developed a concern for a certain girl in the class. She seemed to notice a need rise to the surface. The girl was bursting with potential, but she lacked confidence. Moreover, she seemed uncommonly serious for a sophomore. Deciding to reach out to this girl, Shannon volunteered to correct more essays for the class, hoping that the student's work would reveal some insight into her life. It did, and Shannon prayed for how to comment on the student's writing. After a few essays and an equal number of comments, the student took notice of the kind and thoughtful words written on her work. She felt the compassion extending through Shannon's encouraging responses and decided to talk with her about what was causing her to act the way she did. This student had grown up in a faith-based home but had fallen away from the faith her parents had shared with her. An ugly divorce and several other circumstances had tarnished her picture of faith. Shannon's care of the matter spoke to the girl's heart and eventually led to the student asking others about this teacher and her faith connection. One Sunday the student surprised her teacher by showing up at the church service in hopes of finding Shannon there. Shannon's intentional care played a role in what became an ongoing relationship between that student and her Creator, and overtime a renewed relationship between the student and her family

Like Michael, Kelley, Liz, Sam, and so many others, this student found herself touched by a teacher who was willing to accept the connection between her professional calling and her spiritual calling, recognizing the deep implications of the time spent in the field of learning and caring for the soil. Teachers who do this look and see beyond the temporal value of their work; they internalize its eternal value. They recognize the importance of how their speech, listening, and living speak to the students around them. They ask God how they are to respond, and they follow. Like my grandfather, they recognize their larger role in the work they do. They seek to glorify God in and through that work. They desire to bless those around them. And from time to time God brings them into conversation with others in a remarkable way.

Reflect and discuss:

21. What roadblocks can you imagine threatening to stand in your way of building encouraging connections with students? Together with another person, brainstorm solutions to those challenges.

22. Thinking about the Barnabas story in Acts 9, how can we be "sons and daughters of encouragement" to our students?

23. Consider the suggestion that our speech, listening, and living reach beyond the temporal and into eternal importance. Which words in Scripture can you place on your heart to help you remember this importance?

5

How the Farmer Works the Field

EARLIER IN THE SUMMER (incidentally, the same summer as the tomato fight) Grandpa informed that same cousin and me that we would be planting tomatoes (yes, the very same plants that yielded ammunition for our battle later in the summer). The three of us walked together to the barn, where Grandpa had attached the planter to the back of a tractor, and our training began. We had seen older cousins use this machine in previous years, and from a safe distance it appeared easy to operate. At a closer look, though, neither my cousin nor I felt quite as confident. So we watched and listened closely.

Grandpa showed us the two seats where we would be siting and the shelves that would hold the trays of tomato plants for us to plant. He then explained the process. "Between the two of you are these rubber fingers that turn on a track, as the tractor pulls the planter along. When the fingers open, you need to put a plant between them and let go when the fingers close. If *your* fingers get stuck, you will get planted with the tomatoes. Be careful!" Grandpa looked at us for understanding, and both of us stood there silently with large eyes. Then he went on, "The roots need to go in the ground and the leaves up." He looked at us with a self-satisfied smile, as though he had just told a great joke. "So hold the plants with the roots pointed toward you. You understand?" He stopped and looked again. We had no response but a nod. "Good." He went on, "When you run out of plants in the tray, yell. I'll stop, so you can get more plants off the wagon. Get on now so we can go out to the garden." That was it. Our instruction on this potentially dangerous piece of equipment that could "plant us in the ground with the tomatoes" lasted less than two minutes.

I'm not sure what my cousin was thinking on the trip out to the field, but I was rehearsing my grandfather's words in my head and looking the planter over, thinking about not having my fingers pinched in the planter's fingers. I wished I had asked some questions, but it was too late, and I was too stubborn to admit that I didn't understand something after having told Grandpa that everything was clear. We were heading into the field to plant tomatoes. Suddenly, in the middle of my thoughts, the tractor stopped and lowered the planter to the ground. Grandpa shouted, "Okay, ready? Start planting!" I wasn't sure why he asked if we were ready; he didn't wait for an answer. He simply turned on the tractor's power take-off and slowly shifted into first gear. The rubber fingers began turning, just as Grandpa had said they would. My cousin and I looked at one another and began taking turns placing plants between the rubber fingers, as we had been told. What had seemed so easy suddenly became a game of kinesthetic concentration and rhythm. After a row or two we found that rhythm, and the work slowly became easier. The trouble with easy, though, is that it is where you can become less careful. It is where you lose focus and run into trouble.

The ride on the planter steadily became a relaxing job. My cousin and I started joking and throwing bits of dirt back and forth, because that is what two middle school–aged boys do when the work is easy and they lose focus. That was also our downfall. Up until that point our plants had been perfectly spaced. We hadn't missed a single one. Somewhere in the middle of our third set of trays we stopped looking at the plants and just stuck them in the fingers of the planter. This must have gone on for a couple of minutes, because when I looked up, I saw a good seventy-five feet of brown root balls, rather than the green of tomato plants, standing up out of the ground. My cousin must have seen it at the same time, because when I looked over at him he looked back, and time stopped for just a second. We needed a solution, and fast. Grandpa would not approve of upside-down plants.

Without thinking, I jumped off the planter, telling my cousin to plant for both of us. Running from one plant to the next, I pulled each one from the ground, turned it over, and replanted it by hand. Not wanting the tractor to reach the end of the row before I had finished and returned, I needed to hurry. It worked. Just as the tractor approached the end of the row, I had replanted the last green sprig, dragged my feet to cover the footprints, and jumped back on the planter. Grandpa didn't see a thing.

The rest of the morning's planting was stressful. We didn't dare take our eyes off the job. We didn't talk much or throw any dirt balls. There was no way we wanted to risk another upside-down plant. By the time lunchtime arrived we had planted nearly a thousand tomato plants and our hands were tired and ready for some of Grandma's lunch.

With freshly scrubbed hands we all sat down at the dining room table. Grandma placed the food on the table, we prayed, and the morning was forgotten, as we dug into a casserole of farm-raised surprises. Midway through the meal, Grandpa turned to me while buttering his bread. He asked us how the planting had gone. We were pleased and told him so. Grandpa nodded and took a bite of his bread. He continued nodding, swallowed, sipped some juice, and asked, "What do plants need to grow?" I thought he was joking, but he apparently wasn't, because he took another bite and chewed, still looking at me.

"Well," I said, "they need water, sunlight, food, and warmth."

Grandpa smiled and swallowed. "Where does the water go?," he asked.

Not wanting to beg the question, I simply told him that the roots drank the water from the soil.

"Right," he said. "And where does the sunlight go?"

"In the leaves, Grandpa," I answered. "Why are you asking me this?"

His answer came in the form of a question. "Why did you plant all those tomatoes upside-down then? You had their leaves so they couldn't get any sunlight," he laughed. Grandpa's sense of humor was always dry and hard to detect. "Did you two get to talking and messing around back there or something?"

We both grimaced and admitted that we had, and that was the end of the discussion. Nothing else was said.

Reflect and discuss:

24. *What life story can you remember in which you found yourself in a position like this, thinking you had done the job well only to learn that it had gone wrong?*

25. *How would you respond differently now?*

26. *How can this story speak to us about students in a similar position? How does it speak to us as teachers?*

27. *Imagine a scenario and share it with another person.*

On that particular day my cousin and I had been given a specific role to play in the garden. Grandpa's instructions were to sit on the planter and plant tomatoes. He gave us a specific task with a specific set of instructions with a specific purpose. We had already invested hours into each flat of plants in the greenhouses, preparing the soil, planting the seed, caring for the temperature and moisture of the soil, and transplanting into larger trays. All of that effort succeeded in giving us plants that were ready for transplanting. As was the case in each other step, planting the plants in the garden had a proper method that worked toward the end goal of a good harvest. In order for the plants to thrive and produce a harvest, my cousin and I needed to faithfully play our role in the job.

Planting the seedlings in the ground that day was certainly important. Without it there would be no food later in the summer, but the job couldn't be left there. Each day brought different tasks with different responsibilities, each working toward the growth, care, and success of the plants in Grandpa's garden. Some of those plants were weaker and more fragile than others. Grandpa showed us how to pound wooden stakes in the ground next to them and carefully bind the plants to them so they grow without being blown over by the wind. Some mornings found us running rototillers between rows. Grandpa wanted to keep the soil loose and discourage weed growth in the garden. Then came the dusty, itchy work of spreading straw around the tomato plants after they had caught root. Despite the messy, sweaty work, the effort served to hold the moisture in the ground and protect the plants from soil erosion and caking mud after a heavy rainfall. In dry times we dragged hoses and sprinklers around the field to bring much needed water to the thirsty plants. Each day had its tasks, and depending on the patch we worked, the weather, or the time of summer we needed to be ready to do what was necessary in the garden. This ever-moving cycle of activity holds true for teachers as well, at practical, pedagogical, and spiritual levels, as we do our work in the garden of our classrooms.

Reflect and discuss:

28. *How do you see the cycle of activity shown here finding its application in the classroom?*

29. *Which roles do you see yourself as a teacher playing in the classroom?*

SCATTERING SEED IN TEACHING

CONVEYOR OF KNOWLEDGE

Our first and most obvious role in the garden of our classroom is that of a conveyor of knowledge. God has given each of us teachers a specific category of interest for a reason; he wants us to share it with others. Sharing knowledge and understanding, though, is more than simple delivery of data. It is intimately connected with form and purpose of delivery. Jesus was the master of both. When we bathe ourselves in the Gospel accounts, we begin to soak up the light of Jesus' ministry and teaching. We become the benefactors of his style and method. Jesus taught by story and metaphor. He taught by object lesson, and he taught with the props that were available. Finally, he taught within a context of hospitality.

The stories that Jesus used in his teaching drew in his listeners. What he taught took life into its context and offered layers of meaning. Listeners whose hearts were ready to hear the great depth of the message that a story contained did just that. They heard Christ's deeper meaning. Those who were not ready to grasp the truth of his teaching were nonetheless rapt with Jesus' words. They enjoyed the story and the surface wisdom that it contained. Jesus, using the very same words and stories, spoke to both the spiritually mature and immature. We can find an example of this sort of teaching in Matthew 13. Jesus had just finished speaking to a large crowd near the lake. He had told them about the sower. The disciples asked him in verse 10, "Why do you speak to the people in parables?" Jesus' response is riveting. He looked at his disciples and gave them a straight response. He explained that he used parables that hold the secrets of heaven. The secrets were right there in front of all who heard the story, though not all would grasp the full meaning. Nonetheless, Jesus told the story. These stories were clearly and masterfully told because, between them and his healing ministry, Jesus seldom failed to draw a crowd. We read about one such occurrence in Matthew 14. Jesus had just heard about the death of his cousin John. The Bible tells us that Jesus withdrew to a solitary place. When the boat he had been in landed, though, the crowds were already there waiting for him to continue his work.

Another way in which Jesus taught was by using object lessons from life around him. He used object lessons to create connection between his teaching and the people who listened. Because of the abstract nature of the life view that he taught, Jesus utilized everyday objects and ideas to create an emotional connection with his people. The people who listened to Jesus understood the many uses and purposes of salt. They grasped the importance of light. They could picture a sower casting seed across his field. When Jesus spoke the object did much of his work for him; he didn't need to explain every tiny nuance of meaning.

One example that comes to mind is the day when Jesus saw a woman who had been accused of adultery. The teachers of the law, in an attempt to trap Jesus, asked his thoughts on the matter. Jesus bent over and began scrawling in the dust on the ground while the Pharisees pressed him for an answer. Jesus knew that they were really trying to corner him, and he turned the tables on them, teaching them by using an object lesson. The punishment for the woman's adultery was going to be stoning. The very object that the Pharisees and teachers of the law were wanting to cast (both at the woman and at Jesus) is the one Jesus used in his lesson. The Bible tells us in John 8:7–8, "he straightened up and said to them, 'Let any one of you who is without sin be the first to throw a stone at her.' Again he stooped down and wrote on the ground." In this one imperative sentence Jesus taught a major lesson in theology, social interaction, and spirituality. We know that there was no misunderstanding of his meaning, because when Jesus stood back up the crowd had already begun to disperse. When the crowd had left, Jesus released the woman and invited her to leave her life of sin. His lesson, infused with meaning, also contained an invitation.

Invitation, or more aptly hospitality, may be the most attractive piece of Jesus' teaching. We often hear about the radical miracle of Jesus' multiplication of fish and loaves for the crowds of thousands, and how Jesus cared for the multitudes that followed him to learn. One particularly beautiful example of Jesus' teaching through hospitality was after his resurrection. Jesus stood on the shore one morning watching the results of a disappointing fishing expedition. Some of his disciples, not recognizing him, headed in with their heads low. Jesus asked them if they had caught any fish, and learned what he had probably already known, namely, that there were no fish. He told them to cast their nets to the right side of the boat. When they did their nets came up loaded with fish. One assumption was that Jesus had filled them. What's even more humorous than this is the scene that took place when the surprised disciples finally dragged the overly loaded boats to shore. There Jesus was waiting with a fire and freshly roasted fish. After having reached into the heart of the men's need, he made breakfast.

Reflect and discuss:

30.*How do we look to Jesus to fill our nets or baskets?*

31.*How can we as teachers practice and develop the habits of invitation and hospitality?*

APPLICATION

As we consider all of this, a question arises: How will we model these things of Jesus in our teaching? How, if we teach in a secular setting, do we approach the wisdom that Jesus lived out loud? There is no lack of research telling us about the power of story and metaphor as teaching tools. But the key is in the delivery, in the practical use of life-giving stories and metaphors. Jesus always drove his point home in a way that left his followers looking upward and inward. Where are those examples for us? Which stories and metaphors are we collecting along the way? Which of them affirm and build? Which of them tie in with our teaching and the larger picture of life and eternity? How can we craft them to draw in the ears of our learners and point them to deeper meaning while placing learning within a context? This is likewise the case with object lessons. Where are the teachable moments in the classroom? How can a simple event stand as an illustration for what you are trying to show your class? How can that very same event also quietly convey some moral or eternal principle? Your students' eyes and ears are waiting for you to teach them, and they want you to make it personal for them. They yearn for the learning to be real. They hope that it will be meaningful. Look into their lives. Listen for their interests. Take what is real for them and build on it through your teaching. Give your learners a reason to invest. Make them want to come back . . . hungry for more.

Connected with that hunger is the hospitality Jesus offered. To give hospitality within our teaching we could certainly take the literal route and feed our classes with food, which they would in deed love, but hospitality is deeper. It means more than just food, more than multiplying loaves and fish, more than having a roasted breakfast on the shore. The hospitality that we really want to offer is that which finds us giving of ourselves to our learners. When we reach out to them in love and compassion, caring for their needs, they sense the kindness. They know that we are truly there with them on the learning journey. It sometimes takes simple steps. An example I see in one teacher I know is at once simple and profound.

He greets each student each day upon their entering his room with a kind word and handshake. Then, when they leave, he wishes each of them a good day and a word of thanks for their work in class. A simple gesture speaks to the kids. It also allows the teacher to see into their eyes and sense how they are as they come and go.

Tell your learners that they are important to you. Listen to your students when they talk. Listen beyond the words. Watch their eyes. Look for their expressions. Move around your room and be near them. All of these things that show a guest in your home that you are glad for the visit also show your students that you care for them. This is the hospitality that Christ showed. It showed and it shows that we are scattering more than just academic information. A purposeful farmer is more than a person who tosses seed onto the soil or seedlings into the dirt, and a teacher does more than just scatter bits of knowledge.

Reflect and discuss:

Let's look to the questions in the application section. Answer them for yourself in writing and then discuss them with another person.

32. *How do you draw these concepts into your content area?*

33. *How do you use what you know of your learners to draw their lives and learning together?*

CONNECTORS OF EARTHLY KNOWLEDGE TO ETERNAL PURPOSE

In the sharing of knowledge we need to remember that the fear of the Lord is the beginning of knowledge. Certain types of knowledge are useful for our pursuits here on earth, whereas others are seen as pertaining to our pursuit of eternity. Nonetheless, the ability to acquire any and all knowledge comes from our Creator. It belongs to him. Everything that we have the ability to know is therefore a gift from a gift giver, and all that we teach passes from that Giver through us to our students. For this reason we acknowledge that when we share knowledge, we may give and receive an additional blessing: connecting that earthly knowledge to its eternal perspective and purpose. We do so by connecting what we teach to other disciplines. We do so by presenting in a straightforward and clear manner. We also do it by embedding what we teach into life's larger picture or context, acknowledging the interconnectedness of our subjects to the rest of life and ultimately eternity.

Not all of us teach in a private setting that affords us the legal permission to speak directly about our faith. Nonetheless, we all have the freedom to point what we are teaching and learning to the larger context of life and meaning. Each area of academic study, whether it be art, math, science, philosophy, language, music, or otherwise, is at its base an exploration of or expression of the life and existence God has given us, so let's work with it. First Peter 3:15 does after all remind us to "Always be prepared to give an answer to everyone who asks you to give the reason for the hope that you have. But do this with gentleness and respect . . ."

CONNECTING WHAT WE TEACH TO OTHER DISCIPLINES

It doesn't take much creativity to notice the interconnectedness of one area of knowledge or teaching to another, so rather than presenting our subjects in isolation, let's show the interconnectedness. The bees in my grandfather's garden moved about and pollinated any plant that was flowering, assumedly leaving behind microscopic evidence of one plant visit in the next plant's flower. In this and many other ways all the plants in a garden share with one another. This is also true in learning. You can hardly effectively teach foreign language without referencing the learners' first language, any less than you can ignore the culture, music, art, and beliefs of the people who use the language you are teaching. The instruction of math and science can easily encompass large segments of life and nature and point to the brilliant patterning and cycles that exist in creation. History, likewise, looks at life and the cycles of the human story, drawing in evil and goodness. All academic and non-academic subjects share space and context with all others. Furthermore, looking beneath the surface of the body of knowledge they represent brings us into the myriad possibilities that exist for opening learners up to the mystery of life. We all know these things, but moving from knowing to exercising this reality is key.

One science teacher with whom I spoke stands as a great example. He understood the state required curriculum for earth science and biology, and he took his job seriously, intending to meet and exceed each and every standard and benchmark. His first job, though, was to teach his students the very strict rules of scientific process. He was, after all, a science teacher, and in that role he intended to teach science by the rules of science. This effort was invested in the kids' minds to help them develop discernment in their reading about science and scientific research, but it extended beyond science to life as a whole. He wanted his students to apply the rules whenever they were presented a piece of data. Very specific steps need to be taken to draw from hypothesis, to theory, to fact, to scientific law; and this teacher wanted there to be no mistake in the students' understanding that some data presented as theory is only theory, and that until the full process is met with uncompromising precision nothing can become a scientific law. He taught his students to apply the critical thinking they learned in class to other areas of life. His desire for truth in life formed the foundation of his teaching; he taught the minds that God gave each student to seek for truth. His prayer was also that the discussion of truth would lead kids toward curiosity to seek out the deeper truth behind the mystery of science and what it is really studying. His prayers are frequently answered. It is no uncommon occurrence for kids to approach their science teacher outside of school hours and ask about the theories taught that are often treated as foregone conclusions and facts. Through these discussions a science teacher gets to scatter seed that wouldn't otherwise be possible.

Discuss and collaborate:

34. *Discuss some plausible ways of connecting your subject matter with other disciplines and the benefits you can see in doing so.*

35. *Collaborate with others to brainstorm how your various subject areas can benefit from such work.*

PRESENTING IN A CLEAR, STRAIGHTFORWARD MANNER

When Jesus spoke to people he employed parable and metaphor as tools for communicating truths that some listeners were not yet mature enough to grasp. Listeners who were ready for the deep truth heard it in Jesus' words. Those who could not yet understand the truth until later and those who never would all heard the same words. Everyone heard the same story, but it hit each listener where he or she was in his or her spiritual development. Jesus spoke in a straightforward and clear manner that delivered what each person needed at the time. In Matthew 7:3–5, for example, Jesus was speaking about hypocrisy and the need for a person to first straighten out the matters of his or her own heart before looking toward his or her brother or sister. He very honestly, and perhaps a bit ironically, told his listeners to get the planks out of their own eyes before trying to help others to remove their own particular specks of sawdust. Jesus spoke plainly. He presented his teachings in a way that the listeners and followers could understand. He did not use ambiguous terms or complicated words to impress anyone. He spoke in terminology that listeners could grasp and presented in a straightforward manner. True knowledge has no need of hiding behind a mask of ambiguity or unnecessary complication. It speaks for itself, and Jesus shows us this.

When we are teaching, therefore, we benefit learners when we help them grasp our lessons step by step in clear language. It is important that we present processes in a manner that matches students' ability levels, cultural understanding, and age and maturity level, while challenging them a step further and deeper. It is equally important that we do so in a compassionate and encouraging way that honors their knowledge and intelligence, recognizes the experience that they bring to the learning, and elevates that experience to the point of drawing on it to help make the new learning more accessible. I always have to remember that each area of knowledge is interconnected. Learning is for life—for now and eternity.

Reflect and discuss:

36. *Consider your subject matter. Choose a challenging topic, one that is classically tough for students to grasp. Think of a clearer way to present it and do so, sharing it with another person of another discipline. Ask for that person's response and input.*

37. *Why is this consideration so important? How does our willingness to practice this in our teaching show Christ's light to others?*

MENTORS

Any teaching that we accomplish is contingent on our effectiveness as relationship builders and mentors. Recall when we talked earlier about the soil samples and how each learner in our classes carries a different set of needs! Each student we encounter comes to us with his or her story. Some stories are extremely encouraging; others are very sad, but they are all the stories of the young people who are entrusted to us, and can each benefit from what we have to share. Each represents soil full of potential. The manner in which Jesus lived again places wonderful examples in front of us, as we seek to follow his model in working alongside our learners and mentoring them.

As we discussed before, Jesus spent a lot of time with his disciples. As their mentor he worked with them day after day. In a similar way my grandfather spent numerous hours with me working in the greenhouse and garden, seeding and caring for the plants and soil. He mentored me. We as teachers likewise share vast numbers of hours with our students. During these hours we accompany students, walking side by side with them, guiding and encouraging them in their learning. In many different ways (some large, some very minute) we mentor them. Sometimes this happens indirectly, entirely within the context of our formal teaching. Sometimes it happens in a more direct way, one on one. We develop something that a close friend of mine has; it is a special gift that I call "*beingthereness*." If you type the word on your computer, the spell checker will underline it in red to indicate that it is not a real word. Its meaning is real though. This friend is "there" with students. This "being there" proves to be most important aspect of building relationship. It allows her to mentor. Without "beingthereness" a teacher risks being merely another provider of information, which in turn makes the learner little more than another customer.

When students recognize honest, caring relationship coming from us as teachers, our journey with them becomes all the more pleasant and rewarding. Not only does it move their eyes more toward the lesson that they need to learn, but it is also where mentoring begins. Sometimes this mentoring phenomenon appears to be little more than a picture of an additional adult affirming parental teaching at home and providing another model of what the student already knows. On the other hand, mentoring may extend much further. It may reach into an entirely different realm in which the teacher becomes the voice of compassion for a child who knows none. In any case, the need of the student and the level of relationship that develops will dictate the situation. We as teachers must listen and watch. Regardless of the level of mentorship to which God calls us, we need to understand some valuable aspects of mentoring. Mentoring means showing and pointing out certain facets of life in a way that serves to draw connections and make them more understandable. It means challenging the potential of our students. It means encouraging learners in their journey.

As we learn to see life through the eyes of our students, we gain perspective. Once we learn to see from their vantage point we can grasp what our students can see, and how. Then we are able to dialogue with them and point them to another perspective—a wider one perhaps, or a deeper one. We show them things that can only be seen from a broader viewpoint. As kids open up and share more, we hear about their lives and grow in our understanding of them. We draw connections between what they experience and what they cannot see on their own. Sometimes this is academic knowledge. Sometimes it is experiential knowledge. Other times it is wisdom. It is very much like the day when my grandfather walked with me out into the field to pick up dirt, rub it between his fingers, look closely at it, and smell it. Once he showed me how to do this, I could see the soil for more of what it was. I learned to look from a new perspective. My understanding grew.

Reflect and discuss:

38. *Think back to your time in school. Choose an age, perhaps the age group you will likely teach. What was your perspective on life? How about your friends' and classmates' perspectives? How did you think?*

39. *If the previous question was challenging for you, find someone representing the age you teach or will teach. Ask him or her about life. Compose some thoughtful questions that will get the person talking. Listen well and take notes.*

40. *Now, consider how you can reach out to someone of that age and draw him/her to a broader view.*

41. *Brainstorm with another person one or two scenarios and what you can/could do to make connections.*

As our students' understanding grows, our mentoring field expands from showing to challenging. A caring mentor, like a caring teacher, takes a person's new understanding and challenges it. How will new knowledge apply to life? What needs to change based on new understanding? How will life need to alter? Such questions place a learner in position to think and consider growth, which is, after all, our goal . . . growth and fruit.

Challenge without encouragement, though, can end up in discouragement. So a mentor needs to encourage, just as Paul tells us in 1 Thessalonians 5:11 to "encourage one another and build each other up." Had my grandfather reacted angrily to the upside down plants, I'm not certain how excited I would have been to keep working with him that afternoon. Since he responded in a humorous way, encouraging me in the right direction rather than scolding me, I returned to the field that afternoon determined to improve. In the same sense, we sometimes walk a fine line between encouragement and discouragement in our interactions with our kids. This is true in a group and one on one. Our ultimate goal, after all, is to honor God by being an arrow that points toward him in all that we do, which draws us to our final role as farmers in the field.

Reflect and discuss:

42. When have you been encouraged by someone with authority over you?

43. How did it come to happen?

44. When have you been discouraged by someone in an authority position?

ARROWS POINTING TOWARD GOD

As servants of the living God, we seek in all that we do to be arrows pointing toward God: in our actions, in our words, and in our thought lives. When we do, we scatter seed that God can in turn cause to germinate and produce fruit. We should leave no stone unturned as we search our hearts in this area. Our students watch us, let there be no mistake. They pay attention to our behaviors and our words. We may not recognize it, but they know which teachers care and which teachers could care less. Each day we point kids in one direction or another, either toward heaven or toward hell, by how we interact with them. Since we want to honor God and reflect him, we look into how we do this by how we look and see God and ourselves, and in turn students and our subjects. We do it by how we listen and hear, by how we speak, and by what we do and don't do. Each aspect of who we are gives insight into who we are and what we really believe. Like my cousin and I on the planter that day, our work in the garden either faces into the soil or toward the sun.

SEEING

How I see reflects what is in my heart and soul, what I understand and believe. In Matthew 26:22–23 we read that our eyes are the window to our soul. The point about windows is that they look in *and* out. If my eyes take in images that honor God, my soul is light. If I feed my soul with dishonorable images, though, my soul is dark. Since windows work both ways, I have to consider how I look outwardly at life and how I see God. This is my first focus as a Christian. As a teacher my picture of God influences how I see my students, my colleagues, and my profession.

How do I understand God? How do I look at him? Augustine looks to God's creating us in his image, and one specific outcome of that creation. In book 1, chapter 1 of his *Confessions*, Augustine, speaking to God, meditates, "Thou hast formed us for thyself, and our hearts are restless till they find rest in Thee." When we honestly recognize the truth in that statement and seek God out as our Father, our Creator, our Savior, our Counselor, and our Teacher, we are looking to him with eyes that marvel at what he has done in making us, caring for us, saving us, and offering himself to guide us. We can see our lives as his life, and every aspect of our profession as teachers through his eyes. Until we do, we will be, as the quote states, "restless." Once I realized this and began to talk to the Holy Spirit about the matter, every aspect of my teaching changed. We'll explore the personal side of this more in chapter 6. One teacher I interviewed illustrates the point though.

As a child Jane had dreamed of being a missionary. Her thoughts were that her dreams would lead her to a life of travel. As she matured she came to see missions as something much more vast. She has come to realize that she has, in her words, "a mission to help children become responsible adults who love the Lord and give to him to get their strength from him." This mission did not lead Jane overseas as she had thought it would; it led her into a classroom. After several years of dealing with the meaning of this, Jane came to the understanding that her work as a teacher *was* part of the mission God had given her. Now, as the result of much prayer, Jane understands her mission as two-pronged. On one side, she is commissioned to "lead students through the curriculum and, more importantly, lead them to a life in which they accept themselves and work to reach their potential." On the other side, she tells me that, "Along the way, I hope that, by example, I also reflect for them what lifelong relationship with God looks like." Jane reached this understanding after having taught several years with her eyes focused on "just teaching." She saw her only goal in teaching as that of sharing information and training students in learning processes. Later the Holy Spirit pricked her heart, prodding her to listen to God's voice in her teaching as well. Once Jane found the harmony between her life and her teaching, and heard God's voice speaking to her about teaching, she began to look at herself in a new way. We can all reach this point, and as we do so we understand ourselves in a new light. In turn our profession broadens into what is truly is: a portion of our overall calling.

Seeing God, ourselves, and our profession in a correct light leads us to look at our students with clearer eyes. They are the reason we teach. God has given us life and he has given us work to do in this life—a life that displays beauty, healing, and glory. As teachers we love and honor God, in part, through teaching our students. Seeing these students as the gift that they are is key. We understand that each person we teach is a child of God and comes with a past and a future. When we look at the students in our classes with this understanding, we learn to see past the façade that so many of them wear to school. We see more deeply into their person and grow in compassion for their joy and pain, excitement and anger, acceptance and denial. Seeing deeply helps lower our defenses and personal hang-ups. It places us in a position to realize that teaching is not just an act of speaking, but also one of listening.

Reflect and discuss:

45. Taking on the theme of seeing, and the idea that our eyes are the window to our souls, how do we protect our souls to do God's work as teachers?

46. What are some of the encouraging and some of the discouraging images that are placed before us vis-à-vis our profession and our students?

LISTENING

When I was a growing up, I often heard it said that a person is given only one mouth, but two ears. There seemed to be some allusion to using them in proper proportion. Acknowledging the wisdom in that, though, is a difficult irony to internalize in our profession. Nonetheless, we will talk about listening before speaking.

Teachers are expected to speak well, deliver good information hour after hour, and be prepared to respond to all manners of questions. This is a large part of our training. We learn to build lesson plans and deliver them. We learn to move about a room and make eye contact with our learners and speak so that all feel engaged in the conversation. We learn to master our content so that we can present, show, and speak. What about listening?

Listening often escapes us. Sometimes the prospect of silence can be scary, to say nothing about what someone might ask. What happens when a person asks a question whose answer I don't know? What happens when I'm told something and do not know how to respond? It matters little whether it is a student, a colleague, or an administrator who asks, because teachers sense an internal imperative to KNOW. As a Christian, though, I experience the call to listen (and obey). James 1:19 tells me to be quick to listen and slow to speak. John 8:47 reminds me that whoever is of God hears the words of God. Proverbs 8:13 tells me that it is foolish to answer before hearing. These are hard words to hear, but I need to hear them anyway. If I cannot listen to my students and listen to the meaning behind their words, I have not earned their ears or hearts. If I refuse to listen to my colleagues, the same result comes in a different form . . . all the more so when my ears are not tuned to my administrators. Listening shows caring. It is a passive, yet active demonstration of how we see those around us. It is one of the simplest ways to witness. When we listen, and listen well, we model Christ. When we listen others notice. When we honestly listen we earn an invitation to speak.

A while back God reminded me of this lesson. A particular class that I was teaching was beginning to lose its flare. I greatly enjoyed the students in the class and had known most of them for three or more years. Nonetheless, I found myself struggling to get excited about the class. Anyone who knows me would think it odd that I would have any loss of excitement for teaching anything. In prayer God pointed me to speak with the class directly and then to listen. I did. The next morning I began the class hour with an announcement that we needed to have a class meeting. As I explained my thoughts about how the class was going and asked the students about their thoughts on the matter, they began to open up. The longer I listened, the more they said . . . the more honest they became. The class recognized that I was listening with my heart, not just my ears. Once the conversation about class ended, the students shifted the topic to one about life in general. They began asking questions about college, life beyond college, and relationships. By the end of the class hour, the class (people and subject) not only regained its excitement, but also found new direction and focus . . . on the part of the class and the teacher. God lead me to listen, and in the end he also gave me a new place to speak.

Another example of listening came up in a recent conversation with Edward, a school psychologist. The focus of the discussion was working with student challenges and discipline. Over a course of years he recognized a trend. Certain teachers at points during the year would storm into his office bursting with complaints about one student or another. Their expectation was that Edward, as a psychologist and counselor, would sit down and talk some sense into the student in question. For many years Edward did his best to help. One day, however, this counselor was struck by a question in his mind. He wondered how well the complaining teachers knew their students. So as a result he sat down and composed a list of a few basic questions that a person should be able to answer about another person to show his knowledge of that person. From that point on, whenever a teacher entered his office with a complaint about a student, the counselor took out his list of questions. He would ask: How many siblings does this student have? What are their names? Does the student live with both parents? How about pets? Which pets does this student have at home?

etc. . . . Each of these questions aimed at how well the teacher listened to his or her students, how engaged the teacher was in the lives of the students, how well the teacher knew the students. Did the teacher listen to the learners or just speak and expect to be heard?

Reflect and discuss:

47. *How does listening impact relationship?*

48. *How does listening (or not listening) on the part of the teacher impact the learning that can happen?*

49. *Give good and bad examples of listening that you have witnessed or practiced. How have the good examples instructed? How have the bad examples taught you what not to do?*

50. *How can you build listening into the instruction of your subject and dually reflect Christ and boost learning?*

SPEAKING

When I think back to the days of working in the field with Grandpa, I can't remember him talking very much. Somehow I remember most everything he ever said, though. He spoke when speaking was necessary. He acted when it was time. He responded to questions in as few words as possible. He didn't seem to carry any deep life philosophies that lead him to intentionally use few words. I think that it was just part of his nature, and Grandpa, as I stated before, did not waste words. He said what he meant, and he communicated it clearly. When a specific row of cabbage needed to be weeded, Grandpa took me there, pointed to the row, and simply said, "This row of cabbage needs weeding. If the hoe nicks the plant, it will damage it. I'll be in the bean patch when you're done. Come find me if you have any problems." He then looked at me for a moment to see that I understood, nodded his head, and climbed back on his tractor. Four sentences, a look, and a nod communicated the task. In those four sentences Grandpa gave the necessary information, offered necessary advice, explained the next step, and pointed me where to go for help. He spoke with me, not at me. He watched for understanding, gave me a chance to speak, and got out of the way.

The Bible teaches much about speaking. Ephesians 4:29 reminds us to keep corrupt talk out of our speech and only use speech that builds others us. In 1 Peter 4:11 the matter is pressed even further, as we learn that we are to speak as though God were actually speaking through us. Proverbs overwhelms us with wisdom on how we should speak. James 3 specifically attaches the taming of tongue in speech to teaching. He compares the power of the tongue to rudder on a boat, the bit in a horse's mouth, and a spark. Like all of these things the tongue can work toward good or evil. For teachers there is a deep connection. Our words, our timing with words, and our tone in speaking communicate far more that the meaning of the individual words we speak, much more than the information that we intend to share. They communicate what is in our heart, our hang-ups, our minds. When we speak, those around us listen and evaluate us. They will inevitably evaluate our loyalty to what we profess. They will evaluate the validity of our claims. They will decide whether or not to continue listening.

Janine is a former inner-city high school student. I asked her to tell me about a favorite teacher. The response that she gave me ended up being more than I had asked for. She told me not only about a favorite teacher, but also about her least favorite teacher. During her sophomore year this girl's family had moved into her school from a more suburban school district to live closer to her dad's work in the city. Feeling like an outsider, she depended on her teachers to help her feel connected and cared for. That very same year she encountered two examples, one positive and one negative. The one teacher met her with the gleaming face of a mother. She had been teaching for decades and greeted her students at the door each day with a smile and deep eyes. The way that she spoke with her students conveyed a caring that reminded the girl of her first-grade teacher. Her social studies class was rigorous, but the discussions that the teacher held with the kids gave them trust in her. She asked questions in a strong but gentle tone and listened with her entire body. Her responses to an incorrect answer always drew out something correct before kindly encouraging the student toward a "deeper understanding" or a "different perspective" on the matter.

She used words such as, "I think I understood you, but I need you think about that some more and come back. I need to understand everything." Other times she would correct an answer with, "That was partly right. Let me ask you some more questions and help point you to the rest of the answer." The teacher always looked for a positive manner of encouraging and filling in the blanks in a student's understanding.

Janine's least favorite teacher offers great contrast. He taught literature and "didn't seem to like it." Janine described him as being rough with his students, always wanting to be right, and therefore not very good at listening. Although participation counted a part of the class grade, Janine and others felt very uncomfortable participating in class; they didn't trust the teacher's response to their thoughts. They were afraid that he would "make fun of" them. In Janine's description the teacher would say that an idea was "ridiculous" or "invalid." She didn't look forward to that hour of the day.

How we speak says so much about us. Each of us can think of times in our lives when we have spoken as though speaking the words of God. We can also remember instances when we have set fires with our words. The power of what we say and how we say it challenges us in all areas of life; our classrooms are no exception. As we seek to be arrows pointing toward God, this one area, perhaps more than the others we've discussed, directs the students we meet each day.

Reflect and discuss:

Before moving into the next chapter, let's reflect on the theme of speaking.

51. Brainstorm instances in which you or someone you know has "started a fire" by not being careful with words or the tone of voice used. In retrospect, how can a teacher react differently to build up a person instead?

52. Now think about instances where you or another person succeeded at building up or encouraging through choosing the right words and/or tone of voice. What was the reaction?

Looking back over each of the roles we play as teachers, the task of scattering seed through our teaching may seem monumental. As we consider our responsibilities in sharing knowledge, connecting it to the larger eternal picture, mentoring and pointing students upward, we realize that we can only succeed in any of these to the extent that we grow in our personal walk. That is the subject of our next chapter.

6

Personal Responsibilities of Farmer and the Teacher

EACH AUTUMN, AFTER THE harvest was complete and the last of the squash were sold or given away, Grandpa turned his focus from the daily activities of caring for the plants to other pursuits. The tractors and other equipment and tools had worked hard all summer and needed to be maintained. The greenhouses required cleanup. The barn likewise was in dire need of organization. All of the following year's work in the field could take place more efficiently if this work were also done. Beyond the physical labor involved in maintaining the farm and the tools, though, Grandpa also read about new seeds, fertilizers, irrigation equipment, and planting techniques . . . not to mention the *Farmer's Almanac*. When he was not working in the field, when he was away from his work, he still held the field in the back of his mind. Logging what had been where, how it had grown, how the growing season had gone, Grandpa thought about his work and what he could do for the health of his garden. He read articles by master gardeners and talked with gardener friends. He learned and he shared what he had learned. It brought him joy; he was called to it.

Farming, like teaching, is different from a job. It is a calling, and as a calling it colors the way that a person experiences life. When the farmer is not in the field, he looks at life through farming metaphors and growth cycles. Teachers do the same. Intentionally or not, we think about typical life situations through our teacher eyes. Each story that we share runs the risk of becoming a parallel to school or learning. Each story we hear becomes potential fodder for teaching in the classroom. The lives that we experience in and outside of our work blend together. In order to teach as Christ calls us to teach, in order to see, listen, and speak with Christ-like compassion in our classroom, we carry responsibility in our off time. To grow in our subject area and in our spiritual walk, we need to check our equipment, our barns, and our books in the off-season.

When Christ was not in the field with his disciples, he often went alone up to a mountain to connect one on one with his Father. He regrouped there. He refreshed himself there. When he and his disciples were away from the people who followed them each day, he taught the disciples and prepared them for their further work. The disciples, in fact, went to school for more training to walk as their teacher did. All of this took place outside of the daily tasks of teaching and healing. Reflection on the previous day and preparation for further work happened in the spaces between active work.

Just as the farmer does, and just as Christ and the disciples did, we teachers can look and see our personal responsibilities outside of the field and recognized the intimate link between them and our ability to reflect Christ in the classroom. Sharing knowledge, pointing toward God, mentoring, listening, speaking, and seeing each carry implications that extend beyond our contract hours. They display an understanding that our calling to work in a professional capacity depends on our whole person, not merely the required work time. It assumes that we internalize the overall calling of Christ and see how our personal lives and time, our spiritual growth, and our intellectual and emotional development each inform our activity with our students and colleagues. To honestly walk like Christ in our work it is imperative for us to be ongoing pursuers of knowledge and seekers of deeper wisdom and truth, both spiritually and intellectually. We also need to be prayer warriors in relationship with Christ. For it is in these things that God reaches through us to others with whom we have contact each day.

ONGOING PURSUERS OF KNOWLEDGE

Luke 6:40 (ERV) reads, "Students are not better than their teacher. But when they have been fully taught, they will be like their teacher." The Bible places these words within the context of a lesson on judging others and the responsibility of the believer in being a proper model for those who follow him or her. The appropriateness of the lesson applies itself to this entire chapter, but I will focus it here as it regards ongoing learning.

The Bible tells us that much is expected of teachers. We read in James 3:1–2 that teachers will be judged heavily because of their responsibility, and although the accent in the text appears to be placed on teaching connected with the church, we as Christians fit the mold. Our practical experience in life underlines the idea, even as it applies to a secular context. The contractual basis of our entire profession is the acquisition and sharing of knowledge, understanding, and experience; and in an environment where learning finds itself increasingly centered on testing results, we search for more and deeper ways to make learning and teaching meaningful to life. We therefore sense a multilevel imperative to continue our own learning. We learn because God gives us this ability and the creative curiosity to reflect him. We learn because our profession demands it of us. We learn because a deeper knowledge and understanding of our content renders us more capable of sharing with our learners and lifting them to a higher level . . . beyond standardized testing. When we continue to learn we expand our picture of God's creation and grow in our ability to share it. Psalms 19:1–2 supports that claim in telling us, "The heavens declare the glory of God; the skies proclaim the work of his hands. Day after day they pour forth speech; night after night they reveal knowledge." Our ongoing learning about the creation of God through our subjects brings us to a broader and sharper understanding of his glory. This ongoing learning also grants us the potential of growing and reflecting that glory to and with our students. We travel their trajectory with them, simply at a different stage. As we continue learning, we can better relate to and understand them, and they sense it.

The need for ongoing learning exists irrespective of our content area. No matter what we teach, new knowledge becomes available each year. The study of history and people continues. The interconnectivity of one era to the next, one aspect of life to another, and one region of the world to others on global politics becomes more evident. I am always amazed at the new applications of mathematics to daily life. For example, as a language instructor I would love to believe that our Internet search engines are language based, but it just is not true. They function mathematically. Music, art, language, etc. . . . there is no facet of education that escapes the ongoing trend of research, learning, application, and new knowledge; nor does our learning need to restrict itself to our particular niche. God connected all of creation to all of creation. In the same sense, each new piece of learning that we gather connects us to a deeper understanding of that creation and its purpose, as well as to our students and their passions. To teach is to continue learning.

Pursuing greater knowledge and application certainly places each of us in a better position to grow in our subject areas and to teach, but that knowledge is only as eternally beneficial as the wisdom that undergirds it. I cannot seem to pull myself past the riveting truth that Proverbs 1:7 shares on this theme. "The fear of the Lord is the beginning of knowledge, but fools despise wisdom and instruction." Each time I fall victim to overconfidence in my teaching, these words remind me of where I find knowledge and the wisdom to use it. Years of learning and teaching experience will travel a certain distance, and the acquisition of data will give us the confidence to believe in our ability to share that knowledge. The how, the when, and the why, however, belong to the wisdom that God gives. For this I find myself repeatedly scouring and studying my Bible. Regardless of the struggle, irrespective of the question plaguing me, time spent reading and reflecting always calms me, shows me answers, and clears my eyes.

Reflect and discuss:

"With all of the responsibility placed on a teacher, how is it possible to add ongoing learning to the list?" This is a question teachers sometimes pose.

53. *How do we respond to this type of question when it tempts us? Where are areas of ongoing learning for you? What opportunities exist through reading, classes, online learning, etc.? Search them out and share with another person.*

54. *What is the importance of pursuing these opportunities?*

55. *What role does/should curiosity play?*

Knowledge starts with the fear of the Lord, but it continues and spreads into all areas of life. As teachers we constantly pour ourselves out by sharing what we know. We do it professionally in the context of our work. We even do it sometimes unwittingly among friends and acquaintances. And as the farmer knows, a well that is continuously used needs to be kept full . . . otherwise it runs dry. We refill our intellectual tanks in many ways, and we do so in an effort to remain sharp and current in our knowledge and understanding of our discipline. We do it to gain a deeper grasp of what we study and teach. We do it to grow in our ability to connect what we learn and teach to the One who gave us that knowledge in the first place. Growing our knowledge comes at a price though. It consumes time, energy, and often financial resources.

As mentioned earlier, I teach in two places, both in a publicly funded secondary school and a faith-centered university. Each summer, in addition to personal study and travel, I teach two courses to non-traditional-aged students who take time out of their schedules to return to school. Some of these men and women come to gain a new degree as a shift in their professional calling. Others do so to add an endorsement to their current position. Still others enroll in classes for enrichment and ongoing learning. They engage in the learning conversation with other adults who want to grow in their knowledge and experience by sharing the experiences of others. We laugh and struggle, stretch and listen, study and grow together. The irony for my position in the classes, though it shouldn't seem terribly ironic at all, is that being the instructor of these particular classes actually helps fill me for my full-time teaching.

We live and teach in a time full of opportunities for ongoing education. Open your favorite Web browser and type in search terms such as "online classes," "continuing education," "distance learning [*your subject area*]," and watch your screen become filled with hits that lead you to options for on-ground, online, and correspondence courses in which you can enroll to continue your education. Never before have we seen so many options for continued learning in an institution of higher education, regardless of whether you are seeking to enroll in a single class or working toward an additional degree.

Ongoing education seems to be an obvious choice toward the pursuance of additional knowledge, especially since an advanced degree often offers increased opportunities, but what are some other routes? Right now you are reading this book, which intends to challenge and expand your perspective on our call as teachers. Other books will achieve this effect in other areas of teaching. But we shouldn't stop there. Sometimes adding to your learning takes you in directions that you wouldn't naturally imagine.

A science teacher with whom I spoke is not a science teacher only; he practices what he teaches each year by planting his own fields (metaphor unintended). He has expanded his understanding of God's turning of seasons into a hobby that brings application to all he teaches about weather, growth cycles, plant biology, and life . . . not to mention additional income. A foreign language teacher whom I knew before her retirement spent each second summer traveling overseas, sometimes with students, to work or take part in a missions outreach. While some colleagues joked about her working during vacation, it was clear how powerful that "work" had been. It seeped out in every area of the classroom the following year. A third teacher I know takes his teaching of writing and sets it aside each summer to become the learner and participate in an annual writer's workshop. He maintains that the best way to understand his students is to go where they are and become a student himself.

Many options exist for us to continue growing in knowledge and experience as teachers. One task is to seek them out and gather wisdom on which to pursue.

Reflect and discuss:

56. *Brainstorm options that you can imagine aiding you in knowledge-growth as you pursue your calling as a teacher. Discuss them with partners or with your group.*

SEEKERS OF WISDOM AND TRUTH

Teachers, like farmers, work in all types of weather: sometimes storms of life, sometimes the warmth of educational sunshine, sometimes confusing fog. Regardless of the weather, we need to stand with clarity in front of our students each day. Only God's peaceful calm will allow us to walk along with them, knowing that they will stumble, become frustrated, and want to give up. When we spend time in God's Word and in God's presence, he slowly opens us to his wisdom and truth, and it is there that we gain an understanding for the right mind and heart of teaching. It is there that we deeply sense the importance of Matthew 6:6 telling us to go to our room, close the door, and pray. Likewise, it is in that time of prayer that we open ourselves to God's Spirit to teach us the connectedness between his teaching and our learning, between our learning and our teaching, between our call to teach and the Caller.

Our need for wisdom in education isn't limited to the classroom; we will encounter many difficult times requiring us to respond with the peace and calm that only God's wisdom can give. We are going to run unexpectedly into barriers, specifically as Christians in education. Politics that sometimes stand counter to our worldview will ask for our agreement. Ethical battles will tempt us to take the easy road and compromise truth, rather than follow the path that we know is right. In the uncomfortable case of political and ethical battles, God's wisdom and truth are what we need to give us the will and ability to pull through. When we are pressured to join in an effort that defies our sense of justice and beliefs, we need wisdom to stand strong or risk being blown away.

One afternoon I walked through Grandpa's garden carrying an itchy armload of straw to spread around the tomato plants. Just as I was about to release the last handful, I looked down into my hand and noticed a head of wheat among the straw dust in my hand. I remembered the verses in Psalm 1 about chaff and seed. Bringing my other hand against the first, I rubbed the two together and saw the chaff separate from the seed and blow away in the slightest breeze. Psalm 1 tells us to go to the water and be planted there. It promises that we will give fruit in season. Our time studying Scripture and praying supplies that water and that wisdom. Wisdom shows us what to say when. It teaches us how to see and listen. It gives us discernment when we decide what to do and not do.

I need this wisdom every day, and each day I am thankful for the words in James 1:5, "If any of you lacks wisdom, you should ask God, who gives generously to all without finding fault, and it will be given to you." How I crave more wisdom! Whenever I work with my students, I must ask God to guide me and speak through me. When I do, I realize that it is the time spent alone with God that feeds me, refreshes me, and guides me. I realize this because the words that enter my heart are those that I have read and shared during my time of quiet prayer and Scripture reading. The more time I spend in the garden of God's instruction, the more that God's words will express themselves through my thoughts, my actions, my words. The more I listen, the better I listen. God's Word and Spirit counsel.

We access God's counsel in reading and studying Scripture. We listen to the Holy Spirit and receive guidance when we pray. God also calls us to community with others. One teacher I interviewed sees all three of these options as necessary. His work in school is first and foremost done with students, but he works through the conduit of fellow teachers as well. Early in his career he spent time getting to know his colleagues. He sought out other adults in his building that felt called to pray together and lift up each other and the students in his school. The group, which started with three or four members, slowly grew. This small gathering of colleagues has met weekly to pray for their school. Each of the group's members seeks God's leading, God's wisdom, and God's truth in the calling to teach. They stand behind each other to encourage and challenge, because they all want to grow.

Reflect and discuss:

57. *In what ways has God worked in you to teach you wisdom? How has he worked through others around you?*

58. *What challenges have you encountered in your connection with education? How do you need wisdom to approach them?*

PRAYER WARRIORS

Spending days, weeks, and years with my grandfather meant being in my grandmother's presence as well, and spending so much time with the two of them developed certain expectations in me. Some of those expectations grew into habits. Each morning my grandmother woke early, before the sun. Before anything else crossed her path, she prayed. Her nightstand was covered with devotional materials, including a prayer book and a list of people she knew and didn't know. She prayed for each of them before beginning the physical business of her day. The prayer over every meal concluded with thanks to God that those who were there were together and for the "beautiful weather." Her day was punctuated by periods of prayer, and her day ended with prayer. She was the prayer warrior of the family until her final day. Each of her seven children, each of her brood of grandchildren and great-grandchildren, could go about their day with the peace of knowing that this lady had them covered in prayer before they even woke.

Life in general requires much prayer. Our lives as teachers come with so many twists and turns of conversation, unexpected events, and emotional and intellectual challenges that we require all of the help that we can find. Certainly our own faculties run dry quickly. Prayer is where we talk with God and ask for his direction, support, and strength to do what he calls us to do. It is in our conversations with him that we are reminded of the vastness of our responsibilities as teachers, the lives of the students we teach, the colleagues that we encounter, the community to which we belong. Agreeing with the depth of the importance of prayer Martin Luther is credited with having said, "If I fail to spend two hours in prayer each morning, the devil gets the victory through the day. I have so much business I cannot get on without spending three hours daily in prayer."[1]

Far from being the originator of this idea though, Luther simply echoed Christ's life and practice of regular communion with the Father in heaven. Luke 5:16 shows us a picture of Christ as he

1. Bounds and Chadwick, *Classic Collection on Prayer*, 608.

often went to a mountainside to pray. Mark 1:35 tells us how "very early in the morning, while it was still dark, Jesus got up, left the house and went off to a solitary place, where he prayed." Continuing yet one step further, Ephesians 6:18 underlines the practice for us, encouraging us to "pray in the Spirit on all occasions with all kinds of prayers and requests. With this in mind, be alert and always keep on praying for all the Lord's people." With these pictures in mind, with such encouragement in my heart, and with Christ's example in front of me, I can hardly imagine leaving such an important aspect of my spiritual walk out of my life as a teacher. Far too much relies upon it.

In our prayer time we have a wonderful opportunity to lift up our students, their learning, their lives, their relationships. We can also ask God about how to live well among our colleagues. Each of those lives is so precious, and our presence in education so important, that we can hardly depend upon ourselves to get by on intellect and good intentions alone. God wants us to join him in his work, not ask him to join us in ours. And so he calls us to prayer on how to do it.

In my personal walk in Christ, in my walk with him as a teacher, I continue to learn about the importance of prayer. It has been a long journey full of inconsistencies. I have wavered between times of deep prayerful devotion and times of dryness. After years of struggle, I have realized that my prayer time needs to begin as soon as I shake off the cobwebs of sleep each morning. Before the quiet darkness of the early morning gives way to the business of the day, I find myself talking with God and praying over my family while they sleep. Immediately after that, though, my heart turns toward the day ahead. The Holy Spirit places the tasks of the day in my heart so I can give them to God. I close my eyes and, in my mind's eye, scan the space in my classroom for each class period, asking God to bless each of my students. Inevitably one or more of the students in my class stands out, and I pray for him or her. This work never goes unanswered. On the contrary, on mornings where I allow my busy schedule to distract me, rather than taking time to reflect and pray, something always goes awry. A day placed before

God, on the other hand, always seems to find peace, regardless of the surface outcome. As Romans 11:33 says, "Oh, the depth of the riches of the wisdom and knowledge of God! How unsearchable his judgments, and his paths beyond tracing out!"

The work that God assigns us in the garden is important work. There is much to do . . . too much for us to try and do it on our own strength, by our own wisdom, on our own. If we understand our calling as Christians, if we grasp our calling as teachers, we see that the two are intimately woven together in the same fabric. The gifts that God has given us and the calling that he extends are one and the same, and in serving him in the field and reflecting him there we fulfill part of what he has made us to be. To do so, we prepare for the field, even while we are standing outside of it.

7

Scattering Seed beyond the Edges of the Field

Whether it seems convenient or not, we are teachers, much in the same way that we are Christians; we are called. We cannot separate out our faith from the rest of our existence, any more "than a farmer can separate the color of a carrot from the fact that it is a carrot" (Donald Pickerd). A person who has been called to teach cannot separate the skills and propensities that accompany that calling from who he is and how he is seen.

WHETHER MY GRANDFATHER WORKED in the field, stood in church on Sunday, or enjoyed a farmhouse breakfast at his favorite greasy spoon, he was all of who he was. His name was Don, and he was married to Eileen. They were the couple who sat near the front of church each Sunday. They were the couple who ran the garden and vegetable stand on Leonard Street. They were the people whom everybody knew. When I say that "everybody" knew them, it is only a slight exaggeration. This simple man and his wife worked God's soil together, each doing his or her share of the work, and they shared the abundance of who they were and what they had with more people than I could tell you about within the confines of this book. In our very large family there is a standing joke about being places far from home and encountering random people in casual conversation, only to be asked, "Oh, are you related to Don and Eileen?"

You see, my grandparents' vegetable stand provided their family with much needed income. Their large family saw hard times—times of little, times of great stress—and their work had its functional purpose in providing for their family, much like our work as teachers provides us an income. Their work as farmers, though, also established a portion of their identity within the larger community. They worked hard and had contact with many people through the context of their work, it is true, but there is more. Out of who they were, what they believed, and the work they did also came extra: extra time, extra caring, extra fruits and vegetables. My grandparents shared with others around them. They gave away much of what their large garden produced, and it mattered little whether or not they knew the person receiving the blessing. They shared and spread seed beyond the borders of their garden. They never separated who they were from what they did. They received, and so they gave. The work that they did in their garden was hard, often grueling, and with no guarantee of a plentiful harvest, but they worked the field, brought in what they received, and faithfully shared their blessings.

As I write this book, a large for-sale sign stands in the front yard of that house and garden. The place where the memories and lessons here were created stands now recorded in family history and a couple of local newspaper articles written about its owners. The house and land will be sold. The grandparents who shared their lives with us have gone home to their Father. The tractors and garden tools will be divided among family. The stories will live on though. Seed will continue to be scattered, because of what was scattered by a particular generation.

This is not the end of the matter, though. For in as far as we consider the scope of our professional calling, it is sometimes easy to overlook the larger picture. Though our primary concentration is in the students we teach and encounter, a larger context exists. Teachers inevitably stand out in their surroundings and must, therefore, be prepared to recognize and accept the expanded responsibility. We must consider outreach to colleagues of every description as well as take into account the parent population with which we interact in various ways. There is also the community at large in which we live, worship, teach, and do commerce. At this point the professional life meets the personal life, and one realizes that the various sectors of the Christian life all merge together into one mission: that of God. And we see that being Christians and being teachers are extensions of the same original calling, for God has not only given us gifts, he also has equipped us with the capacity to spread seed in all areas of life for his glory.

Reflect and discuss:

59. Take the proposition of connection between our calling as teachers and our original calling as members of God's church. Look to Scripture and find some verses that support it. Reflect on them. Share and discuss them.

In the midst of day-to-day activities and business, it is easy to be tricked into thinking that our seed-scattering influence stops at the door of our classroom or the edge of our school property, that our role and title of teacher remains there behind us when we leave. To believe that is a mistake though. Not to seem overly grandiose, but our influence reaches far beyond our immediate classrooms or even the physical property of the school. Many teachers live in and near the communities in which they teach, and so their identity follows them into those communities. They do commerce there. They worship there. They entertain themselves there. They in fact are a part of the fabric of the community, beyond the school. Wherever they go in public, they are known and seen, at least in part, as teachers by the people who know them. This thought causes some teachers to shudder; it is seen as a quiet violation of their identity as a private person. I see it differently, because my calling to teach comes from God. It is a part of my entire person, and that person is called to reflect Christ where he is. I welcome it, and rather than attempt to separate my professional identity from my perceived private identity, I prefer to simply allow the one to be part of the whole. For if I attempt to separate the various aspects of my identity, i.e., as a teacher and or as a Christian, I run the risk of affirming the accusation that, "We live in our own insular world, never making the effort to move beyond the confines of 'Fort God,' never daring to experience life among those who do not believe in Jesus. We do not listen. We do not empathize. Instead we preach from afar."[1] If I sequester my "teacher" identity to school and my "Christian" identity to church, then I refuse the wisdom of the parable of the sower.

SCATTERING SEED ALONG THE EDGES OF THE GARDEN

If this is all true, how do we work through our calling as teachers and our identity as Christians and move as positive models among colleagues, especially if we work in institutions that draw a heavy line between religion and state? There is nothing lofty or mysterious about this, but it is something that we need to consider. Teachers often experience a temptation to close the door to the world and escape into the kingdoms of their individual classrooms, and it is understandable. The classroom is where our focused work happens. It is there that we meet and learn with the students we teach. In our rooms we sense an ability to direct the course of events. Beyond the doors, though, are hallways connecting us to others with the same tasks, the same work, and we can choose to build relationships with them or not. And in as much as we are called to glorify God by reflecting Christ to the students in our classrooms, we show him to our colleagues (or not) by how we interact with them.

The most likely time to meet with colleagues is during lunch and planning times in the day; this is also the most challenging time to meet with them. When teachers gather during their lunch or during planning time, a negative "shop talk" often surfaces. There is often complaining about students, about administration, about other teachers, etc. At this point we reach a place of decision. How will we react? Will we play along? Will we change the topic? Will we leave and avoid working and eating with these people? The example seems petty and small, but how we as Christians choose to react in situations such as this is more important than one might imagine. Remember what James 3:5–6 tells us about the tongue?

1. Dickson, *Gospel according to Moses*, 196.

Likewise, the tongue is a small part of the body, but it makes great boasts. Consider what a great forest is set on fire by a small spark. The tongue also is a fire, a world of evil among the parts of the body. It corrupts the whole body, sets the whole course of one's life on fire, and is itself set on fire by hell.

Martin, one of the teachers I interviewed, actually spoke to this topic. Early in his career Martin chose to avoid unnecessary social contact with colleagues whenever possible. He didn't like the negative conversation about students and the backbiting discussion about parents and administration. His took a defensive stance to protect himself by eating lunch alone. As time passed, though, Martin began to recognize that this approach wasn't working. First of all, it isolated him from his colleagues, which placed him in a weak position in terms of building relationships. It also caused Martin's colleagues to talk about him behind his back. They thought that he was smug, believing himself to be better than them. Little by little, though, he realized the damage that his self-imposed separation was causing, and he began to intentionally interact with fellow teachers. He decided to join them in the staff lounge for lunch once or twice each week, no matter how uncomfortable it was at first. Martin even went to the extent of bringing homemade treats to share with colleagues periodically, which bent the conversation in a different direction. As he came to know this small group of colleagues better, God opened his eyes to something that had been there all along, but which his closed eyes had not been able see. The fact was that, regardless of worldview differences, Martin shared many similarities with his fellow teachers.

As time passed, Martin made a connection and realized that building relationships with his colleagues required the same care as those with his students. He began to listen to colleagues in the same way he listened to his students, and as he did so relationships grew. After a period of time his coworkers began to lower their walls. They realized that they had misjudged him too. Martin built closer relationships with a couple of colleagues in particular. Becoming a better listener, he learned about some struggles that one of his neighboring teachers was experiencing in life. Martin began to pray for this person and he looked for ways to encourage him. Through this small intentional shift in one man's perception, relationships changed in his small corner of a school building. Space opened for Christ to be seen. Martin learned what Christ taught in his life. He learned that a candle hidden under a basket cannot shine any light that can be seen. He also learned that he was not an island; there were Christian brothers and sisters who also wanted to grow and reach out. Essentially, what we all know intuitively Martin learned practically.

Reflect and discuss:

60. *Martin's story is an easy one to imagine, but what will you do when the answer isn't as easy to navigate, when the situation is more than a simple shift of habit and perception on your part?*

61. *What are some circumstances with colleagues that may cause a much heavier challenge to you?*

EXAMPLES OF SEED SCATTERING BEYOND THE FIELD

One afternoon not very long ago I walked into my town's public library with my family. As I reached for the door to open it for two students who were leaving, they both smiled at me and thanked me. Once they thought they were out of earshot, one of them said to the other, "Hey, that's the _____ teacher." The short interaction made me smile.

Three aspects of that contact seized my attention. The first was that I did not know the students. They were two among over two thousand members of our student body, nonetheless they knew me and something about me. The second thought-provoking point is that their first association with me was my professional title, the "_____ teacher." Finally, there seemed to be some reason that they felt my presence noteworthy enough to point it out to one another. Though I was not on or near the school property, though I was not wearing typical work clothes (rather, shorts and a t-shirt), though I was with my family, I was first identified as the "_____ teacher." My titles of husband, dad, church member, community member, coffee shop–goer, etc. were of little concept to these kids. "That's the _____ teacher."

John, a teacher living in a smaller outlying community, related a similar situation with me, with the exception of place. One evening he arrived at a local restaurant to meet some friends for dinner. Upon entering the building and asking for a table, he was met with the call and hand wave of a group of parents whose students had been in his class. Needing to wait a while until his table would to be available or before his friends would arrive, he walked over to the group flagging him down. The first words he heard were an invitation to join the "gang" while he waited. The conversation began with school, meandered to life in general, traveled through the worlds of sports and politics, and ended again where it began, with education. This gentleman noted that no matter how far the conversation wandered into other areas of interest, it always returned to the reminder of his important tie to the community. Indeed he was a private citizen wearing several hats, but his one defining hat in the eyes of that particular group was his role in the lives of the young people he taught. It defined him, to some extent, in an important way.

Not all teachers experience life in this manner though. Unlike John, Amanda lives and teaches in a large urban area. The school where she teaches is a tough place to be; home, for many of her students, is even tougher. Amanda rented an apartment with a colleague from her school. For their safety they intentionally found one in a different neighborhood than the one served by the school. Each day, Amanda and her roommate traveled to and from school together, expecting safety in numbers.

Amanda's love for her students shone through in her teaching and her interaction with her students. She worked hard to connect with them and learn what she could about their lives beyond school so that she could better relate to them. She prayed for them, and she told them about that fact when it was appropriate. One day Amanda walked into a coffee shop in the strip mall near her apartment. Sitting there alone in the corner was a girl from one of her classes. When Amanda approached her, she expected the girl to be bothered about a teacher talking to her in public. This girl was the one who had given her the biggest struggle in class. What

Amanda encountered that evening though was a different person. Her walls of protection were down, and her eyes lifted. Surprisingly, she asked Amanda if she wanted to sit down and talk. As the conversation moved along, the student lowered her barriers even more and told Amanda about her mom's addiction and how she stayed out late every night. The girl knew what her mother was doing to earn money, but she shielded herself from thinking about it too much. In reality, she stayed away from home as late as possible because she felt unsafe there. This conversation led to others and to Amanda becoming the person whom the girl would call and check in with each night. She needed someone who knew where she was and when. Amanda's seed scattering expanded.

One spring Robert sat across the table from two parents at conferences. Their daughter had slowly changed from the cheerful, loving, and compassionate little girl that she had been in elementary school into someone they could no longer recognize. As Robert listened he began to see his role as teacher morph into that of listener and, to some light extent, counselor. Before him sat two adults who loved their child, lost for answers. They were looking to the teacher for ideas. He did, after all, see their daughter several hours each week, and had done so for three years. What did he think? What advice did he have? Would he pray for them and their daughter? What they did not know was that he had already been praying for her. As he shared that information with them, they sighed, and the mother began to cry.

Each of us will encounter our own picture of seed scattering, depending on our teaching context and our connection with the community in which we teach. It may be that your home of worship is near your school so that you encounter students there. Perhaps you only infrequently bump into the kids from your school (or their families). It is also feasible that you constantly find yourself in interaction with the people in your school because you shop, eat out, worship, and generally participate in the same community as your students and their families. Regardless of the level of contact that you have with these people, you scatter seed each time you see someone at the mall, in the coffee shop, at the store, in church, or on the street.

Reflect and discuss:

62. *Think about some of the teachers you know. How do their identities as teachers extend into the communities in which they live?*

63. *In what ways can their community connections as teachers be a conduit for sharing Christ in their larger communities?*

64. *What challenges can you imagine arising from this?*

Our lives as teachers (though the title is not our identity) are closely wrapped up with our identity in the eyes of those around us. Regardless of where we are, what we are doing, and how we are speaking, the people who know us through our professional calling consciously or subconsciously process our mannerisms. The way we live either agrees or disagrees with how we present ourselves in our classes each day. More importantly than that, though, is the fact that we are Christians who teach students in classrooms each day and live with some level of contact with the communities surrounding those schools. If the way we live agrees with the way Christ loves us, we scatter seed of beauty and healing; we glorify God. If it disagrees, we scatter seed that will produce weeds.

At the point at which our professional lives meet our personal lives we come to the knowledge that the Christian life—all of it—belongs to God's one mission. Christians who teach live out their professional and private callings for the same purpose and with the same strength. As stated before, God has given us gifts, and he also has equipped us with the capacity to spread seed in all areas for his glory; and in that sense, everywhere we are and go we are seed scatterers.

Final Thoughts
How Do I Start Scattering Seed?

READING ABOUT OTHERS' ENCOUNTERS in education and thinking through them is one matter. It is quite another to think through them and imagine ourselves scattering seed. This is especially true for those working in a publicly funded or business educational setting. If we remember Christ's words in Matthew 22, when his disciples asked about the greatest commandment, we are reminded that loving the Lord our God is first, and that loving our neighbor is second.

Do I as a teacher show Christ's love by encouraging those around me through what I do and how I do it? If I do, this becomes a tangible picture of Jesus. How does my face appear? Is it full of dark clouds, or does the joy of faith in Jesus show in my eyes?

In all areas of my life I need to honestly acknowledge my shortcomings and show a willingness to grow through and from them. This displays humility to my students, my colleagues, my neighbors. Christians are often viewed by people of other worldviews as prudish and self-righteous, neither of which offers an accurate image of what we believe. Sometimes the most difficult step to take is the step toward humility, especially as a teacher. I am expected to be the expert, or so I think. I've learned from my students, though, that they already know I'm not perfect. When I am willing to show them in real ways that I also understand this reality, they are much more willing to not only learn from me but also share and grow with me. This is no different with colleagues. It is very difficult to be real around a person who refuses to do so himself. Can I communicate to my students that I will not know the answer to every question asked, but that we will find the answers to some questions together and celebrate together? Am I willing to acknowledge that as a teacher I am still on the learning trajectory of my subject matter (just like my students are), but I am simply further along and have more experience?

What about integrity of planning, preparing, assigning, and evaluating? Knowing my students and building trusting relationships with them is one important piece of reflecting Christ. It is another to take that knowledge and build it into my planning and preparing for my students. I need to build lessons that translate my understanding of my learners' needs into a careful, fair, and encouraging introduction of the subject that I teach. I must keep my eyes, my ears, and my heart open to their successes and struggles to help each student move forward at an appropriate pace in an encouraging way. None should be left to struggle alone. Furthermore, am I evaluating the learning in my class in a way that reflects real use of the subject matter? What steps am I taking to honor my students through careful evaluation? Am I looking out for all of my learners, not just those who are easy to teach and learn with excitement? How am I reaching out to the students who would rather not be there and make life difficult? How about those who vehemently disagree with who I am and make it known?

Moving beyond my comfort zone to grasp the wisdom of the Good Samaritan and its implications for us as Christians in a diverse world of ideas and worldviews lets others see that, regardless of whether our beliefs agree or disagree with lifestyles, the love of Jesus penetrates by teaching us to love all around us. I recently listened to an interpretation of the parable of the Good Samaritan that differed in some important ways from others that I had heard in the past. We often hear about the distinction that Christ made among the three examples of passersby in the story. There is the highlight that it was the enemy of the stranger on the road who stopped to help him. Often the priest and Levite are attacked for not helping the man, but then excused because helping him might have made them ceremonially unclean. The problem is that they were both coming from the temple and therefore not needing to concern themselves with that matter. The real matter is that they both refused to concern themselves with someone about whom they knew too little. They might have dirty themselves with someone else's refuse. They might have "caught what he had."

Christ made it clear that regardless of who is near or far from us, each person is a neighbor. As teachers we hold a large role of influence, and we can love our neighbors as Jesus loves sinners, as we have been, or we can refuse to do so. In addition to the students, this means that the neighboring teacher with an entirely different approach to classroom management, and life in general, is my neighbor, and I need to love him or her and look for a place to share grace. It means that the student who openly rails against everything that I hold true and sacred is my neighbor. This person also needs to receive the grace that God extends to me through Jesus, because I also have been the disbeliever.

Teaching is a tremendously challenging calling to receive; it is also a wonderfully rewarding one. As a Christian teacher I find myself daily forced to make choices that will represent Christ or not. For nearly twenty years God has been working in my teacher heart to challenge me, grow me, and test me. It is my prayer that what he has taught me through these stories of colleagues and students, through the many seasons of planting, weeding, and harvest, will bless you and encourage you, as well as challenge you as you go out and scatter seed.

One more story; it is a short one.

Both of my grandparents are gone from this earth now, as I have already said. At both of their funerals, roughly seventeen years apart, some common messages were shared by family, friends, acquaintances, and neighbors. One was a memory of their ongoing generosity to everyone around them. They shared the abundance of their harvest, no matter how large or small. Another was a picture of the garden that they both endeavored so hard to grow. The third was their undying faithfulness in serving. Each season of their lives commanded its own form of service, from youth to old age, but in each season they served.

My prayer is that your greenhouse is filled with well-fertilized soil, that you look over your field each new year and learn about your soil, that you care for your equipment and continue to grow and learn in and out of season, that you spread seed in and beyond the field, and that you do it all for the glory of the Master Gardener while you teach for him. I also pray that the stories, reflections, and discussions shared and encouraged here will help you and others around you to look to the many ways we can scatter seed, regardless of our context as teachers.

Reflection and Discussion Questions

CHAPTER 1

1. Reread the last few sentences and think about them. When is it hard to recognize what they are suggesting and apply the lessons to our work?

CHAPTER 2

2. How does society as a whole appear to view education?

3. How do you view it?

4. What values and goals does education appear to have?

5. What expectations are placed on it?

6. How do you understand all of this tying into us as Christian teachers?

7. Reread this last paragraph and consider its suggestions. What evidence do we see of this today?

8. How can Christians prepare to respond?

9. How can we as teachers take a detailed walk around our field each season to gain a deeper feel for what it holds?

10. What are some Scripture verses/stories to hold in mind as we remind ourselves of the importance of teaching as Christ?

CHAPTER 3

11. Brainstorm and discuss some practical ways that we can look at the soil of a classroom to understand its content?

12. How can the students be directly involved?

13. How can it be done indirectly?

14. What stories can you share about the students you have encountered? Where have you been pleased, surprised, heartbroken? Which soil-type does each represent?

15. How could your story affect the kind of soil you are today? How could that story enrich that of your students?

Let's take the questions at the end of the paragraph above and apply them to our own situations. The first question revisits an earlier matter, but the second draws us a step further and points us to our next chapter.

16. How does the steady increase of peer group influence play a role here?

17. How can a responsibility to build the soil be blended into the academic responsibilities of the teacher?

CHAPTER 4

18. What examples of teachers from your past can you share to illustrate worldview projection via how that person/those people live, speak, listen, and act?

19. How/why is it important to maintain a strong consciousness of the connection between our outward living and what it reflects of us and God?

20. What about your mannerisms and words transmit your what you hold to be true and sacred? What do they say?

21. What roadblocks can you imagine threatening to stand in your way of building encouraging connections with students?

Together with another person, brainstorm solutions to those challenges.

22. Thinking about the Barnabas story in Acts 9, how can we be "sons and daughters of encouragement" to our students?

23. Consider the suggestion that our speech, listening, and living reach beyond the temporal and into eternal importance. Which words in Scripture can you place on your heart to help you remember this importance?

CHAPTER 5

24. What life story can you remember in which you found yourself in a position like this, thinking you had done the job well only to learn that it had gone wrong?

25. How would you respond differently now?

26. How can this story speak to us about students in a similar position? How does it speak to us as teachers?

27. Imagine a scenario and share it with another person.

28. How do you see the cycle of activity shown here finding its application in the classroom?

29. Which roles do you see yourself as a teacher playing in the classroom?

30. How do we look to Jesus to fill our nets or baskets?

31. How can we as teachers practice and develop the habits of invitation and hospitality?

32. How do you draw these concepts into your content area?

33. How do you use what you know of your learners to draw their lives and learning together?

34. Discuss some plausible ways of connecting your subject matter with other disciplines and the benefits you can see in doing so.

35. Collaborate with others to brainstorm how your various subject areas can benefit from such work.

36. Consider your subject matter. Choose a challenging topic, one that is classically tough for students to grasp. Think of a clearer way to present it and do so, sharing it with another person of another discipline. Ask for that person's response and input.

37. Why is this consideration so important? How does our willingness to practice this in our teaching show Christ's light to others?

38. Think back to your time in school. Choose an age, perhaps the age group you will likely teach. What was your perspective on life? How about your friends' and classmates' perspectives? How did you think?

39. If the previous question was challenging for you, find someone representing the age you teach or will teach. Ask him or her about life. Compose some thoughtful questions that will get the person talking. Listen well and take notes.

40. Now, consider how you can reach out to someone of that age and draw him/her to a broader view.

41. Brainstorm with another person one or two scenarios and what you can/could do to make connections.

42. When have you been encouraged by someone with authority over you?

43. How did it come to happen?

44. When have you been discouraged by someone in an authority position?

45. Taking on the theme of seeing, and the idea that our eyes are the window to our souls, how do we protect our souls to do God's work as teachers?

46. What are some of the encouraging and some of the discouraging images that are placed before us vis-à-vis our profession and our students?

47. How does listening impact relationship?

48. How does listening (or not listening) on the part of the teacher impact the learning that can happen?

49. Give good and bad examples of listening that you have witnessed or practiced. How have the good examples instructed? How have the bad examples taught you what not to do?

50. How can you build listening into the instruction of your subject and dually reflect Christ and boost learning?

51. Brainstorm instances in which you or someone you know has "started a fire" by not being careful with words or the tone of voice used. In retrospect, how can a teacher react differently to build up a person instead?

52. Now think about instances where you or another person succeeded at building up or encouraging through choosing the right words and/or tone of voice. What was the reaction?

CHAPTER 6

53. How do we respond to this type of question when it tempts us? Where are areas of ongoing learning for you? What opportunities exist through reading, classes, online learning, etc.? Search them out and share with another person.

54. What is the importance of pursuing these opportunities?

55. What role does/should curiosity play?

56. Brainstorm options that you can imagine aiding you in knowledge-growth as you pursue your calling as a teacher. Discuss them with partners or with your group.

57. In what ways has God worked in you to teach you wisdom? How has he worked through others around you?

58. What challenges have you encountered in your connection with education? How do you need wisdom to approach them?

CHAPTER 7

59. Take the proposition of connection between our calling as teachers and our original calling as members of God's church. Look to Scripture and find some verses that support it. Reflect on them. Share and discuss them.

60. Martin's story is an easy one to imagine, but what will you do when the answer isn't as easy to navigate, when the situation is more than a simple shift of habit and perception on your part?

61. What are some circumstances with colleagues that may cause a much heavier challenge to you?

62. Think about some of the teachers you know. How do their identities as teachers extend into the communities in which they live?

63. In what ways can their community connections as teachers be a conduit for sharing Christ in their larger communities?

64. What challenges can you imagine arising from this?

Bibliography

Bounds, Edward M., and Harold J. Chadwick. *E. M. Bounds, The Classic Collection on Prayer*. Gainesville, FL: Bridge-Logos, 2001.

Carlson, Dwight L. *Who'll Be In Heaven & Who Won't?* Bloomington, IN: West Bow, 2012.

Chesterton, G. K. *St. Francis of Assisi*. New York: George H. Doran, 1924.

Dickson, Athol. *The Gospel according to Moses: What My Jewish Friends Taught Me about Jesus*. Grand Rapids: Brazos, 2003.

Erikson, Erik H. *Identity and the Life Cycle*. New York: Norton, 1980.

Freire, Paulo. *Pedagogy of the Oppressed*. New York: Continuum, 2000.

George, Timothy, Denise George, and John Albert Broadus, editors. *Baptist Confessions, Covenants, and Catechisms*. Nashville: Broadman & Holman, 1996.

Guinness, Os. *The Call: Finding and Fulfilling the Central Purpose of Your Life*. Nashville: Word, 1998.

Janssen, Karl-Heinz. "Was für ein Glück, daß die Menschen nicht denken." *Zeit* 30 (July 18, 1975). Online: http://www.zeit.de/1975/30/was-fuer-ein-glueck-dass-die-menschen-nicht-denken.

Kershaw, Stephen. *A Brief History of Classical Civilization*. Philadelphia: Running Press, 2010.

Köstenberger, Andreas J. *The Missions of Jesus and the Disciples according to the Fourth Gospel: With Implications for the Fourth Gospel's Purpose and the Mission of the Contemporary Church*. Grand Rapids: Eerdmans, 1998.

Lewis, C. S. *The Abolition of Man; or, Reflections on Education with Special Reference to the Teaching of English in the Upper Forms of Schools*. New York : Macmillan, 1947.

Newbigin, Lesslie. *Foolishness to the Greeks: The Gospel and Western Culture*. Grand Rapids: Eerdmans,1986.

Palmer, Joy, Liora Bresler, and David E Cooper. *Fifty Major Thinkers on Education: From Confucius to Dewey*. New York: Routledge, 2003.

Palmer, Parker J. *The Courage to Teach: Exploring the Inner Landscape of a Teacher's Life*. San Francisco: Jossey-Bass, 1998.

————. *To Know As We Are Known: Education as a Spiritual Journey*. San Francisco: HarperSanFrancisco, 1993.

Senior, Donald, and Carroll Stuhlmueller. *The Biblical Foundations for Mission*. Maryknoll: Orbis, 1983.

Smith, Christian, and Melinda Lundquist Denton. *Soul Searching: The Religious and Spiritual Lives of American Teenagers*. New York: Oxford University Press, 2005.

Smith, David, and Barbara Maria Carvill. *The Gift of the Stranger: Faith, Hospitality, and Foreign Language Learning*. Grand Rapids: Eerdmans, 2000.

U.S. Department of Labor, Bureau of Labor Statistics. "American Time Use Survey Summary." News release, June 24, 2015. Online: http://www.bls. gov/news.release/atus.nro.htm.

Van Rheenen, Gailyn. *Missions: Biblical Foundations & Contemporary Strategies*. Grand Rapids: Zondervan, 1996.

The Westminster Shorter Catechism. Online: http://www.westminsterconfession. org/confessional-standards/the-westminster-shorter-catechism.php.